Jungung

Jack McGinness

Caution

This book includes images and names of deceased people that may cause distress to Aboriginal and Torres Strait Islander People

Jungung

Jack McGinness

Plaiting the Grass for family, community & the Future, 1902-1973.

by

Kathy Mills

With

Dianne Koser & Matthew Stephen

First Published in 2019

This book is copyright. Apart from any fair dealing for the purpose of private study, research, criticism, or review, as permitted under the Copyright Act, no part of this publication may be reproduced by any process whatsoever with the written permission of the publisher. Inquiries should be directed to the publisher.

© Kathy Mills & Matthew Stephen 2019

GPO Box 4766, Darwin, Northern Territory, 0801.

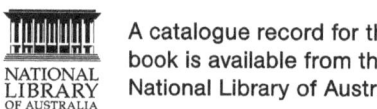 A catalogue record for this book is available from the National Library of Australia

ISBN: 978-0-6484575-1-0

Cover Images

Front: Jack McGinness, c 1950s. (Lockwood, D., NTL, Douglas Lockwood Collection, PH0501-0366.)

Back: Jack McGinness addressing the Australian Council of Trade Unions Congress, Melbourne, 1951. (Unknown, Mills Collection.)

Layout and design by Uniprint, Charles Darwin University, Darwin NT 0909 Australia

Printed in 2019

Contents

Dedication .... **vii**

Acknowledgements .... **viii**

Chapter 1   **Introduction: *Ngirrwut*** ***1***

Chapter 2:   **Stephen McGinness: The Family Patriach** **8**

Chapter 3   **Life at the Lucy Mine** **16**

Chapter 4:   **A New Life in Darwin During the 1920s** **34**

Chapter 5   **Katherine: The House That Jack Built** **61**

Chapter 6   **World War II** **81**

Chapter 7   **Post World War II: The Fight for Rights** **96**

Epilogue: Jack McGinness's Legacy **125**

Bibliography **140**

'The worth of an individual is clearly in their doings.' K. Mills

This is the story of a man and his extraordinary life.

From tribesman to tradesman, and Bridge Carpenter, and campaigner for equal rights.

>John Francis (Michael) McGinness
>
>A man of courage, a man of strength
>
>This man was purpose bound,
>
>His body straight, his voice was strong
>
>His history spans this land
>
>Freedom was his prime pursuit
>
>Injustice was his foe
>
>Courage was his armour. Equality his goal
>
>He never faltered in his step, his mind alert and true
>
>He did not let his own adversity destroy fair attitude
>
>*K Mills*

Dedication

The earliest summons heard by Jack would have been the voice of his mother Ulngindubu calling '*Jungung*', (son).

So I dedicate 'Jungung' to the following people and ideals:

- The memory of *Ulñyunduboo* Lucy McGinness, his Kurrung (mother) calling for him.
  My Wetji (grandmother)
- To *Numundoork* and *Ulmundoork*, old men and women, the ancestral custodians for *Lok Koongurrukuñ*. (Spiritual keepers of *Koongurrukuñ* land, Jacks' place of birth.)
- To Jack's involvement in the National Aboriginal Advancement League, the highly controversial political process that resulted in the inclusion of Aboriginal people in the census of Australia through the 1967 Referendum.
- The legacy of recognition of citizenship rights for the Aboriginal people of Australia including voting rights that saw the liberation of Aboriginal people from institutional life.
- The freedom to live with dignity as equals under the United Nations Charter of Human Rights
- Knowledge for future generations to recognise any form of discrimination and constitutional racism.
- The freedom to speak out against oppression,
- Confidence to oppose and resist any form of racial bias.
- To his family, their legacy is the honor of knowing his personal commitment and the role he played in the process of achieving citizenship rights for Aboriginal People of Australia.
- We therefore acknowledge his personal commitment and dedication as President of the Half-caste Progress Association in the Northern Territory while being involved with the 'National Aboriginal Advancement League'.

Acknowledgements

Original Manuscript, 2003: Acknowledgments & thanks

Kathy Mills, OAM

This book is the result of a project which I started when it was realised that a photo of Jack McGinness was absent from the line-up of past Presidents of the North Australian Workers Union.

Acknowledgement and thanks go to Rob Hitchcock of the Miscellaneous Workers Union who supported the project. Early research work was done by Didge McDonnell and Kootji Des Raymond and a suitable photo was found in the Archives but sketchy details prevented further work. As a member of Jack's family I was approached to write a caption to support the photograph. It was during my research for appropriate words that I realised how important the background story was. As a result, the original purpose got lost along the way and instead through the encouragement of so many people that I spoke to, I have written this story about Jack.

In particular when I approached Peter Spillett, a renowned Darwin historian, his immediate response to recording Jack's history was 'It is a story that should be told'. While sharing his knowledge about Darwin Mr Spillett recalled a conversation he had with Jack regarding Mindil Beach. Mr Spillet said Jack had told him that the word *mindill* was the word for the little edible nut grass that grew in the area. The *Koongurrukuñ* word for that particular grass in Jack's language is *ngulput* and in *Guringi* his wife's language is *Kinnewru*.

I would also like to acknowledge a small Northern Territory history grant that enabled me to purchase a computer to begin this work in its early stages of development which involved researching and recording interviews with people who knew Jack McGinness. Most of his earlier acquaintances and fellow workers like Jack had passed on which made the task a bit difficult while battling with an old computer that had seen better days. In addition I was extremely grateful for the support from the Indigenous Training Centre (Darwin Regional Centre for Employment Program) for providing the necessary technology and equipment enabling young *Koongurrukuñ* in documenting and recording their family history and language *Nguñ Koongurrukuñ*.

I would also like to thank my family for their assistance, knowledge, photographs and memories that add interest to this book. I acknowledge my sisters Sadie Ludwig and Mim McGinness and Joan Angeles as the *Pongoh* people, fire stockers, whose trust in me to write was compelling. I apologize to Mim for the times I called on her as a liaison between myself and Ida Bishop which must have caused her to fuss at times but fuss she did in the nicest way. Thank you to Sadie, who if not for her trust in my ability this book may never have been written. I thank my sister Joan for her help in finding precious football photos showing Jack in the lineup for the Buffalo Football Team. Together their enthusiasm and encouragement was important to me personally and the driving force that led me to complete the work. *Munggung (*cousin) Ida Bishop is the eldest of the McGinness family of *Kungurukan* who lived her early childhood at *Mugidirbirr*. Ida provided important historical memoirs and photographs of the period and the area that was and still is *Mugidirbirr*. We recognise Ida's dedication in preserving the *Koongurrukuñ* language and her personal effort that resulted in the Dictionary *Nguñ Koongurrukuñ*. The dictionary is a monumental effort and should be recommended for a literary award. Ida has created a vocabulary and uniformed structured guide to spelling and unique phonics "The *uruk* or utterance" specific to *Koongurrukuñ* language. I must also mention my son Robert Mills who by using the spelling produced an audio/visual interactive CD ROM using *Koongurrukuñ* speakers in the McGinness family for the voice over. His in-depth knowledge of the language and the fluency of speech are invaluable to the preservation of *Nguñ Koongurrukuñ* and a lasting tribute to his Great Grandmother *Ulñyunduboo* and other elders. Shared anecdotal history is a treasure trove of memories so important in documenting family history and is invaluable to all. Thank you all for your contributions and the important knowledge significant to our cultural heritage. The power of *ngirrwut* is in sharing knowledge and history of our people and our land '*Lok Koongurrukuñ*'. It remains the everlasting attachment to the Indigenous patchwork of the Land Australia.

There are so many people who held Jack in high regard and careful consideration has been taken to mention but a few who played a significant role in his life. These include Allan Smith, Kelvin Gardiner, Fred Laughton, Hilda Muir, Uncle Billy Muir, Bob Henness, Dorothy George and Sheila Clarke. In acknowledging these people it is not to say that the others are less important nor forgotten, they remain in our treasured memories as Jack's friends. I am grateful to those whom have contributed to the script with written works and their own anecdotes and photographs. Thanks must be given to all those people who contributed to this account of Jack McGinness and his life; their comments are very much appreciated while their memories all add to Jack's story.

Many thanks go to my friend Di Koser who endured my highs and particularly my low periods but who was always there ready to help in any way that she could. I appreciate her expertise as a teacher and her invaluable assistance in reading and appraisal of this work.

Jungung

Ngoondjook   News, tidings, message

Kimak   Good, right, proper.

Final publication 2019: Acknowledgments & thanks

I am forever grateful to Di Koser and Matthew Stephen for their enormous assistance given so generously to publish *Jungung*. I would also like to thank Robyn Aitken and Peter Caust for their assistance with the proof reading.

I am particularly indebted to Di for her friendship, support and encouragement throughout this project. I must also sincerely thank Matthew for his expertise and professionalism over the last 12 months that was invaluable in getting *Jungung* to print.

Di and Richard Koser, Mossman Gorge, Queensland, 2018.

Matthew Stephen, National Portrait Gallery, London, 2017.

Acknowledgements

Co Author's Note

Dr Matthew Stephen

This book has had a long genesis. Di Koser began work with Kathy Mills to create the original manuscript in 2003. In late 2018 Kathy asked me to consider the original manuscript with a view to get it to print. Although I came to this project recently my connection with Kathy goes back to 2009 when, as Manager of the Northern Territory Archives Service Oral History Unit, I conducted an oral history interview with Kathy documenting her life story. During the six months this interview took to complete we developed a good rapport based on a shared passion of Northern Territory history. Since that time I have met with Kathy intermittently to discuss all kinds of Northern Territory history topics. I also developed a deeper understanding of the nature and importance of oral history.

The original 2003 manuscript was very much a written account of Kathy's memories of her father, Jack McGinness, combined with stories others had told Kathy over the years. Although not a verbatim transcript it was written very much as it was related to Di by Kathy. Having worked in the field of oral history for over 12 years I recognised that like so many oral histories Kathy's oral testimony and memories were not necessarily in chronological order or contextualised to the extent that someone not familiar with Northern Territory social history would immediately understand.

Over many meetings and discussions with Kathy and with her permission and constant collaboration I began to reshape the manuscript. We agreed that the book must be easily understood by someone who was unfamiliar with Northern Territory history. One way to do this was to reshape the narrative into chronological order. The other important task would be to link the narrative by including some additional contextual historical information.

As far as possible I have retained Kathy's 'voice' that was captured so well in the original manuscript. To do so I have retained the original text as far as possible. As this process evolved it was interesting to see where Kathy's memories and understanding of her father's life were most vivid. Kathy was born in 1936 and so it should be no surprise that her own memories of her father from this time to around the mid-1950s were very strong. Equally Kathy's knowledge of her family history going back to her Grandfather, Stephen McGinness and Grandmother, Lucy *Ulñyunduboo* and her own father's early life prior to 1936 was also very vivid. This can be attributed to Kathy's own character as one of the McGinness family's 'keeper' of stories which takes a lifetime of listening to family stories and their telling and retelling. Kathy discusses this herself in the introduction. Consequently chapters one to six are largely written in the first person where Kathy is telling her story. Kathy's memories of her father's later life are not as

Jungung

detailed and consequently I have provided more contextual historical information chapters seven, eight and nine and Kathy is most often referred to in the third person in these chapters unless directly quoted.

Oral history has its own dynamic that differs from a more conventional history. Alessandro Portelli's, *The Death of Luigi Trastulli and Other Stories: Form and Meaning in Oral History*, is a seminal oral history text. His approach resonates with me because of all that I have learnt while working with Kathy.

Portelli pinpoints where oral history, memory and historical evidence converge. Not something that all historians are comfortable with:

what is really important is that memory is not a passive depository of facts, but an active process of creation of meanings. Thus, the specific utility of oral sources for the historian lies, not so much in their ability to preserve the past, as in the very changes wrought by memory. These changes reveal the narrators' effort to make sense of the past and to give a form to their lives, and set the interview and narrative in their historical context.[1]

Oral history has its own 'truth' and must be understood as such. For those who wish to understand and learn more of the background to Northern Territory social history I hope that the bibliography will provide a useful starting point.

I hope that the combined effort of Di and myself to bring Kathy's history of her father and family does justice to a remarkable man and a remarkable family.

Language Use

Many writers have tied themselves in knots when it comes to language use when talking about Indigenous people. It is a difficult and complex area particularly when Aboriginal people tell their own story.

Official and social contemporary language use about Aborigines and other non-White people was almost always hurtful and derogatory during the period covered by this book. The legislative record is erratic. Some statutes used the noun 'Aboriginals', some used 'Aborigines'. Government reports routinely used 'blacks', 'natives' and 'Abos'. When referring to people of mixed descent, 'coloured' was a common term. When mixed descent included an Aboriginal parent, 'half-castes', 'part-Aboriginal', 'quadroon', 'three-quarter caste' and 'octoroon' were some of the terms used.

Social usage was, and is, different. Because this book is based largely upon Kathy's oral testimony she uses the language most familiar to her. Consequently language that some people may be seen as offensive is just every day to others. 'Whites',

---

[1] Portelli, *Death of Luigi Trastulli*, 52.

Acknowledgements

'Blacks', 'Whitefellas' 'Yellafella' and 'Blackfellas' are part of the vernacular. Many people still make the distinction between 'Aboriginal' and 'Coloured'.

When discussing language use with Kathy we agreed that it was essential that her 'voice' is retained as far as possible. Furthermore we also felt that hearing, or reading, how Aboriginal people talk about their own history is educative in itself and indicative of the times. While it is acknowledged that this may be offensive to some it is not intended as such.

To acknowledge the importance of Aboriginal language to Kathy's history Aboriginal words and names have been italicised. The orthography of Indigenous languages is complex and has changed over time. Kathy opted to use the spelling found in Ida Bishop's dictionary, *Nguñ Koongurrukuñ*.[2] If words were not found in *Nguñ Koongurrukuñ*, Kathy spelt them phonetically. The original word use in Kathy's own poems and the creative works of others has been retained.

---

2 Bishop, *Nguñ Koongurrukuñ*: Speak *Koongurrukuñ*. Ida is Kathy's cousin. Ida is the daughter of Harry Edwards and Margaret McGinness, Jack McGinness's sister.

Jungung

UNION JACK

How ironic:

>That he was christened John which invariably becomes Jack;

>That Jack was to join and became a conscientious supporter of the union movement in Darwin;

>That the Union Jack was the official standard of the Commonwealth that denied him his heritage as a son of a British Subject;

>He was later to become President of the North Australian Workers Union - a branch of the Trades and Labor Council of Australia;

>Much more ironic was the fact that he advanced to the position as President of the Union which enabled him to liberate his people with the full endorsement of the Trade Unions of Australia; and

>Most ironic and much to his annoyance but ironically appropriate he was often referred to as UNION JACK.

K Mills

Chapter 1

Introduction: *Ngirrwut*

My cultural name is *Mooradoop*. *Mooradoop* is the peaceful dove. *Mooradoop* in *Koongurrukuñ*, identifies the boundaries of *Koongurrukuñ* land and all our neighbours; *Larrakia, Woolner, Minitja* and I know them all. This was entrusted to me by my forbearers, something they foresaw in me and that I would do my duty.

I believe history lives with you. It's a generational exchange of knowledge. It's up to the individual how they absorb it and protect what they hear. This is not an Aboriginal thing. It's a human process.

Ngirrwut (passing on) is a *Koongurrukuñ* concept. It was passed on to me by my father and my mother. *Ngirrwut* is hard to define but in part, it is your knowledge, your experiences, your stories, your history that has been passed on to you and your responsibility, your duty before you leave this earth to do everything you can to ensure that your *Ngirrwut* is passed on for the continuation of the story. In a sense it is your will and testimony. While *Ngirrwut* is a duty, it is also an honour.

This book is based on my memories and the stories told to me of my father and those who knew him. My oral history is not only mine but my family's. That is not to say that all my family and those who know us would tell exactly the same oral history. While the details of oral history may differ from person to person the heart of the story rarely does. If this book tells a story that differs from others it is because that is how I remember it. It is up to others to tell their own story.

My *"Ngirrwut"* includes the time I spent with my father Jack when he was President of the Half-caste Progress Association and President of the North Australian Workers Union here in Darwin. In doing so I truly hope that I do justice to the memory.

This story tells of a man who recognised through his personal experience the disparity that existed between Aboriginal and non Aboriginal people. When he gained confidence he went head first into battle to change the status quo. He was 21 years old when he joined the Union in 1923 but by then he was a man who was both respected and admired for his determination in the fight for equality.[1] His courage in dealing with his own adversity as an oppressed person was recognised by his people and he became an advocate in his own right. Throughout his fledgling years with the Union movement he dedicated his efforts towards the Labor Party platform that promoted workers rights. Jack knew that Aboriginal people didn't have social rights let alone worker's rights so he continued to support the Labor Party to promote and improve rights for Aboriginal workers. 32 years later, in 1955, against much opposition from other political powers and persuasions Jack became the President of the North Australian Workers Union within the Northern Territory Branch of Trades and Labor Council in Darwin. This was an historic ground breaking feat.

He was elected to the position at a time when he and other Aboriginal people of mixed race descent were challenging the Federal Government to abolish the *Native Affairs Act* that denied Aboriginal people basic human rights and attempted to control all aspects of their lives. The *Native Affairs Act* was blatantly racist in design and discriminatory towards a particular section of the Australian population.[2]

It was claimed that the *Native Affairs Act* and the Assimilation Policy were necessary for the protection of Native Australians. However, citizenship rights were denied to all Aborigines.

The purpose of the policy, as then stated, was to promote a smooth passage to assimilation and integration of Aboriginal people into society. However, little effort was made to nurture the actual process. Jack observed that the failure of the assimilation policy was the absence of an appropriate community education program.

Through his personal experience Jack found the legislation to be contradictory according to the influence of his father's teachings 'That all men are equal'. Mixed race people or part Aborigines were identified and discriminated against according to the colour of their skin and their lineage to their Aboriginal family. Jack regarded the concept of part Aborigines abhorrent and that change was needed.

The National Aboriginal Advancement League started in the 1930s but was interrupted by World War II. By the 1950s there was a resurgence of interest

---

1   *People*, 4 September 1957. Jack joined the North Australian Industrial Union (NAIU). This became the North Australia Workers Union (NAWU) in 1927 when the NAIU merged with the Northern Territory Workers Union.
2   State and Commonwealth legislation related to Aboriginal people through history went through many name changes. As is common in oral history one common usage emerges within communities as an overarching term. In the Northern Territory and Kathy's experience this is *The Native Affairs Act*.

in the Northern Territory while momentum was gathering in southern states. Aboriginal people around Australia were calling for equality and freedom from the bondage of Commonwealth and State policies. Aboriginal people and other Australians marched and rallied, and formed delegations and demonstrations in other States to express their objections.

Darwin was no exception and a rejuvenated Jack took to this like a duck to water, so to speak. He saw the opportunity to pick up what he and others had started pre war while incarcerated in Kahlin Compound and under the control of the *Native Affairs Act*.

I feel extremely privileged to have experienced the most critical political era for Aboriginal people knowing my father played a significant role in what was known as 'The Struggle.'

Jack became the President of the Darwin Half-caste Progress Association in 1951 in line with the southern state's resurgence of the Aboriginal Advancement League calling on the Federal Government to abolish the *Native Affairs Act* and for equal rights for the Aboriginal people of Australia. Interest was growing throughout Australia and the initiatives such as the demonstrations gained the support by non-Aboriginal people. Around Australia people demanded that Aboriginal people be fully recognised and looked upon as equals in their own country.

In 1957 the National Aboriginal Day Observance Committee, (later the National Aboriginal and Islander Day Observance Committee) was established. The demonstrations and celebrations that continue each year were formed out of these earlier demonstrations in recognition of Aboriginal prior ownership of Australia. The 'agenda' included the adopted slogan 'Pay the Rent' as one demand highlighting the disparity that exists between mainstream Australia and the Indigenous people. Calling for full citizenship rights for Indigenous Australians and declaring Australia Day as Invasion Day and a day of mourning is another strong demand. The rationale was human rights and 'A fair go Australia.'

A referendum was called and on the 27th of May 1967 to vote on the question to empower the Commonwealth to legislate for all Aboriginal people and to allow them to be counted in the census. Australians responded with a resounding "Yes" vote. This meant that Aboriginal people would be included in the census validating their rights as citizens to vote in Federal and State elections.

Jungung

"The right to be, is a Human Right

To be right, is honourable to Humanity"

K Mills 1992

Delegates to the FCAATSI Annual Conference, Canberra, 1967. Included are Doug Nicholls, Joe McGinness, Bert Groves, Harry Penrith, Charles Perkins, John Moriarty, Bill Onus, Clive Williams, Gladys Elphick, Faith Bandler, Jack Hassen, and Alick, Merle, Andrew and Esmai Jackomos. (Unknown, Mills Collection). Note: This caption from; Bandler, Faith. *Turning the Tide,* 83.

Jack's youngest brother Joe who settled in Cairns, Queensland, after his release from the army, was elected President of FCAATSI (the Federation Council of Aboriginal and Torres Strait Islanders (Queensland)). FCAATSI was a very vigorous working group of Aboriginal and non Aboriginal people who lobbied the Federal Government with very strong support from the Waterside Workers Union. It is appropriate to also mention the work of two brothers, Milton and Arthur Liddle, whose activities focused on Central Australia. Their support and involvement extended the boundary of representation of Aboriginal people in the Northern Territory. The legacy of the Liddle's involvement is very evident in Aboriginal services in Alice Springs and surrounds.

The story that was the man.

Jack was a man of obvious talents and good humour. Despite his own personal experience with adversity, he remained fair minded and a very proud and loyal Australian. He was a staunch supporter of the Trades and Labor Council and was known to vigorously oppose any foreign interest groups that threatened external control or ownership of Australia. Throughout his entire life he dealt with difficult discriminating situations which were at times very cumbersome yet he didn't lose sight of basic human rights. He didn't renege on anything he initiated but instead remained steadfast completing all he set his mind to do. Jack was known to back the under-dog through his commitment to right the wrong which threatened to deny basic human rights to so many people. His sense of fair play was obvious through the sports he played and work that has been acknowledged in various ways. Strong language was never part of his speech. If he was extremely annoyed he would yell 'Blast and set fire to the bloomin' thing', 'Cast it forth into the outer darkness', 'God-sufferin' Tom cats' or 'proper no good eh.'

He was slow to anger. That's not to say that he did not at times fly off the handle or fight but it had to be an extremely serious issue. I remember one incident at a Buffalo Football Club "do" at Rapid Creek when a young service man on being introduced to Jack responded in "Pleased to meet you Jacky". After several attempts at requesting that he correct his approach the young man persisted in referring to Jack as Jacky. The reference to Jacky was an abbreviation of "Jacky Jacky" a disparaging term commonly used when referring to any "full blood" Aborigine as being dim-witted or Myall. On the third occasion the young man found himself flat on his back and Jack re-iterating, 'The name is Jack not Jacky".

Many of his philosophies, spoonerisms and sayings will be expressed as we journey along the path he set for his children to follow. A way of life clearly defined with pride in one's identity as the catalyst for strength of character and self-preservation.

Jungung

Whether on hunting trips or throwing the cast net along the beaches Jack remained calm and capable. I remember walking behind my father on the beach at Two Fella Creek carrying a hessian bag for the day's catch. At times when all were tiring he used to chant a little encouraging rhyme as a reminder of the need to press on.

> "You go to work, to get some money, to buy some food, to give you enough energy,
>
> to go to work, to get some money, to buy some food, to give you enough energy,
>
> to go to work, to get some money to buy some food to, etc etc."

He would quote to children who were over enthusiastic about making their wishes known, "If wishes were horses beggars would ride." When questions were asked of what things were or of what was its use, he would answer, "It's a Wing Wong for a goose's bridle" / or something like "it's a constantonotion of a cononstadiddle." The children didn't fully understand the phrase but the way it was put seemed to satisfy their curiosity.

Jack's philosophy could be summarised in a few phrases.

> "Any work that is worth doing is worth doing well."
>
> "A fair day's work deserves a fair day's pay."
>
> "Young men working with adult men should receive a man's pay for what was regarded as a man's work."

These issues were part of his platform as conscientious trades and labor campaigner along with his mate Don Bonson and the formation of the post war Darwin Apprenticeship Board. There seemed to be nothing that could deter Jack from speaking out about issues and doing something about it.

Equality and social justice issues influenced Jack's passion to speak out based on his earlier experiences when his life was totally controlled by the *Native Affairs Act* that rendered him helpless to be an independent person.

Introduction: Ngirrwut

This show was really all-Australian

MELBOURNE aborigines last night entertained Mr Jack McGinness (right), ACTU Congress delegate from Darwin, and singer Harold Blair, who leaves on September 22 to continue his studies in America. Pastor Doug Nicholls is operating the movie projector; the show was in the Mission Hall, Fitzroy.

The Herald Sun, 5 September 1951.

Chapter 2:
Stephen McGinness: The Family Patriach

Stephen Joseph McGuinness, was born in New York Harbour (United States of America) in 1854. Stephen initiated dropping the "u" from McGuinness for personal reasons. According to family oral testimony this was because he thought this may deter the authorities from tracking him after he jumped ship in Brisbane. Whilst Bernard Stephen (The eldest son of Stephen Joseph), retained McGuinness, John 'Jack' Francis, Valentine 'Val' Bynoe and Joseph 'Joe' Daniel all adopted the McGinness surname.

Stephen died in Darwin, Northern Territory on 22 October 1918. He is buried in the Pioneer Cemetery, Goyder Road. As patriarch of the McGinness family his legacy is based on a life that instilled in his children his enduring conviction that everyone is equal, regardless of whomever they may be. He believed that there is good in all people, black and white and that change will come if we come together as a nation.

The full history of Stephen Joseph McGuinness is not known. The McGinness family oral testimony is encapsulated in Kathy Mills, 'Ode to Stephen Joseph McGuinness.'

Ode to Stephen Joseph McGinness

A Catholic man from Ireland
Of Dublin City fame
A sailor from a merchant ship
McGinness was his name

He came here to Australia
To Brisbane's sunny shore
He heard that gold was being found
And thought that he might score

He jumped the ship at Brisbane
And surely made his way
Across the barren country
To where his treasure lay

He stopped at Charters Towers where
He worked with a construction gang
The railway platform being built there
Is where he signed his name

He travelled on to Darwin
A very weary man,
The gold that he was searching for
Was never to be found

He worked on Gulnare Jetty,
Stone mason was his skill
Around the harbour foreshore,
Just down below Fort Hill

The rocks were quarried locally,
And a retaining wall was built
And when that job was finished
He started working on "The Track"

The railway line was being built
So Stephen packed his gear
And went to work for the railways
To bring civilization nearer

Jungung

He worked the railway siding
At the 34 mile peg
That's where he met his lady
The woman whom he wed

Her name was *Ulñyunduboo*
His *Koongurrukuñ* tribal bride
She bore four sons and one girl child
With Stephen by her side.

Then there was a fatal accident
While Stephen was in charge
So not wanting to stay working there
He caused his own discharge

He decided to take his family,
Away from all the fuss
And with the help of Lucy
They headed for the bush

On the way to Bynoe Harbor
While Lucy walked the goats
She found a rock that looked real strange
So she took it back to Mac

He very quickly summed it up
So very glad within
He knew full well the rock she found
Was very rich in tin

He set about to work that land
His treasure to proclaim
With love and dedication
He named it "The Lucy Claim"

K Mills 1984

Railway Wharf, 1887. (Foelsche, P., NTAS, Foelsche Collection, NTRS 3420/P1/9).

Beginning of a long journey

Details of Stephen Joseph McGinness's arrival in Darwin or how he was employed is not well known. Family oral testimony says he was employed in working on the railway embankment leading to the railway wharf which is better known as Stokes Hill Wharf today. Later he gained work on the Darwin to Pine Creek railway line that was constructed between 1886 and 1888. Stephen McGinness was the ganger at the fettlers' camp at the 34 mile peg. It was while he was at the railway fettlers' camp at the 34 mile peg that he met his future wife, *Ulñyunduboo*, who was of the *Koongurrukuñ* clan, of *Koorinjoo,* who are custodians of the Finniss River in the Fitzmaurice region of the Northern Territory. At the time a relationship between Stephen Joseph McGinness, an Irish Catholic and his wife Lucy would have been an offence attracting a penalty of imprisonment or a fine or both.

It was these circumstances that shaped so much of Jack McGinness's life because from birth he was classified by the authorities as being of mixed race descent and categorized as half-caste. The term Half-caste was used to classify Aboriginal persons who were born as a result of cohabitation between a white male and an Aboriginal woman and having brown pigmentation of the skin. Those with fairer complexion were Quarter Caste or Quadroon while others with yet fairer skin and blue eyes were Octoroon. The different pigmentation determined one's category which is now recognised as highly discriminating, offensive and unacceptable under the United Nations Charter on Human Rights. To those who are not aware of the Northern Territory's history it may seem incredible to think that humans could be categorised in such a way based on the pigmentation of their skin. However, to those families who have lived their lives in the Top End it is common knowledge.

Despite the discriminatory legislation designed to ban relationships between non-Aboriginal and Aboriginal couples Stephen and *Ulñyunduboo* began a family at the 34 mile. Jack McGinness was born on the 20th of March 1902. The 34 mile was a section of the railway line that ran between Darwin and Adelaide River. That area of Jack's early childhood is now submerged under the Darwin River Dam. Eventually, the end of the line would reach Birdum where the building of the line connecting South Australia was suspended due to a lack funds in 1929.

Amongst some family papers I found was Jack's first attempt at writing his biography that read; 'On the 20th of March 1902 a child was born with a head on him like a boar pig and a mouth almighty and a bawl rather than a cry'; which he felt was appropriate. We laughed about it because that was his unassuming way of expression, not to draw attention to himself. My thoughts regarding the introduction may have been responsible for discouraging him to write more which is a pity, but I rather think it was a thought rather than a real attempt at writing his biography.

The McGinness family grew at the 34 mile. Jack, his sister Margaret and Valentine were all born there before the family relocated to the Bynoe Harbour area where Joe was born. It is not clear where Jack's brother Barney was born but it could have been the 34 mile as well. Jack was born into a way of life at the fettlers' camp at the 34 mile peg. It seemed inevitable that Jack would eventually work on the railway in later years and this certainly happened. He worked for the railways roughly 20 years, from the birth of his eldest child Joyce in 1926 until after the end of the war in 1945. Life at the 34 mile was his early childhood experience living with his father and the beginning of his life's journey.

The Fettlers' Song

Oh come along down the railway track a fettling we will go
Down the track to an iron shack with a hearty heave and ho ho ho
With a hearty heave and ho

A healthy life I'm a promisin' lads tho' your work is never done
You'll rise and shine in the early morn' and you'll rest at the set of sun, oh yes
And you'll rest at the set of sun

There's ironwood sleepers to be cut There's a rusty adze to hone
You'll run the bolts and check the points and you'll flag the engine down my boys
You'll flag the engine down

You'll pack the sleepers one by one for her wheels to glide upon
And when the ganger calls heave ho you'll pull together as one oh yes
You'll pull together as one

The section cars are there to ride the Fairbanks or Casey Jones
You'll run the length of a Sunday morn
Oh a railways life is fun me lads
A railway life is fun

You'll lift and pack you'll bend your backs
You'll ram the dogs down deep
You'll keep the line straight as a die and you'll rest in the noonday heat, I say
You'll rest in the noonday heat

For its Leaping Lena's sake you see
She's the pride of the north you know
'Cause she bears her load like a regal queen
And it's for her we'll strain our bones, we will
For her we'll strain our bones

She's the pride of the railway crews me lads
As she snorts and struggles through
She's worth your best and all the rest
When she carries her cargo through, hoo hoo
When she carries her cargo through

Jungung

Oh a railway life ain't grand my boys
As you scrub bash the whole day through
But it's worth the toil if you take the call
You'll be proud you gave your all, oh yes
You'll be proud you gave your all

For it's not all fun I'm apromisin' lads   there'll be heartache and sorrow too
But when the payday comes along
You'll drink to an OP brew hoo hoo
You'll drink to an OP brew

So come along down the railway track
A fettlin' we will go
Down the track to an iron shack
With a hearty heave and ho ho ho
With a hearty heave and ho.

K Mills 1989

Telegraph repairs held up by the train at the 35 mile wash out.
(Unknown, Maxwell Collection).

Life on the railway was determined by the rhythms and work routines of the railway itself. Each section of line was identified in miles for the purpose of maintenance work and each section had a gang whose responsibility was to 'run the length' as it was termed. This meant clearing and maintaining safety of the railway line north and south of their respective fettler's camp. The first gang started at the two and a half mile shed at Parap where the railway workshops and loco sheds and train depot were situated. The first length began from the Parap Siding to Darwin Railway Station and Hornibrooks' where the turnstile for the locomotives was situated and south to the 10 mile Knuckey Lagoon.

The next section was from Knuckey Lagoon to the 22 Mile, now known as Wishart Siding, then from Wishart Siding to 34 mile etc. The 'running of the length' was a daily requirement. Each section was called a siding and was equipped with small fettler huts, a quad shed and a ganger's hut. The ganger's hut had an in-call telephone line used by the Road Master when he needed to contact the ganger on important matters. The ganger contacted the office there with a device that hooked up to the telegraph lines enabling the ganger to communicate with the Road Master. The ganger had the responsibility to maintain the section plus overall management of the gang, keeping the time sheets, and financial expenditure.

In later life during his time away from his land and working for the railways Jack never forgot his landmarks taught to him while living with Stephen McGinness and *Ulñyunduboo*. Working for the railways gave him the opportunity to travel to and from Darwin with concessions for his family. On these occasions he would call the children out on the platform at the Darwin River pumping station to call out to country and identify as *Koongurrukuñ* family. This was to identify his children and himself to his country by 'touching' the ground. A point of interest on the journey to Darwin was the ruins of the old 34 mile Fettler houses where he and his family were born. The last sight of interest was the break in the tree line just past Coonawarra East, the Naval base, when we could sight Kings Table across the harbour, the top of *Koongurrukuñ* country.

It was during the time that Stephen and *Ulñyunduboo* were living at the 34 mile that there was an incident on the railway that would forever change the fate of the family. A man was accidentally killed at the 34 mile siding while Stephen was in charge. Authorities determined Stephen responsible so we understand he was sacked for 'dereliction of duty.' Being placed in a compromising situation he left with his family and journeyed across the land back to the Bynoe Harbour mining fields to find work.

Chapter 3

Life at the Lucy Mine

Pongoh Pongoh people. This image was used in the Finniss River Land Claim by Val McGinness who recognised the body markings as *Koongurrukuñ*. (Unknown, NTL, Ronald Lister Collection, PH0135/0056).

'Always was always will be *Koongurrukuñ*': Finnis River Land Claim 1981.

Birthing Place
Nourished by sweet clear flowing water
Offspring of *Nungulukoo* the river
Protected by majestic White Cedar trees
Place of birth of *Ulñyunduboo*
Spiritual presence of Ancestral family
Feeling of peace
Secure
Power of *Mookununggunuk*
Koongurrukuñ story of Survival
Kemek!

K Mills

Stephen McGinness and *Ulñyunduboo* set out on the journey to Bynoe Harbour. On the way *Chugudah*, who was a cousin to *Ulñyunduboo*, spotted a rock that she was carrying and took it to Mac, as Stephen was often called. *Chuguda* had experience with other miners in the area and got to know how to recognise the different rock formations. Mac knew at first sight that the rock was rich with tin and he decided to explore the area. The place was known to *Koongurrukuñ* people as *Mudgidirbirr* and it fitted in with *Ulñyunduboo's* plan to teach her children their culture and take them back to her homeland where they would be near to *Tjupunuh,* her place of birth.

Mudgidirbirr was where her children could grow up in *Koongurrukuñ* country with billabongs bearing her name and that of her sister-in law, a secure place that nurtured the cultural environment close to *Koorindjoo,* the centre, rich in *Koongurrukuñ* heritage. This was the main dry weather camp for *Koongurrukuñ* on the Finnis River and close to their spiritual landscape. At *Mudgidirbirr* Jack and the family was closer to their tribal area and the centre where Jack's responsibilities to land and his people lay.

Life was ideal for a young boy of the era – hunting, fishing and learning about country "*Lok Koongurrukuñ*" and his obligation to land. *Mudgidirbirr* was a proven fertile place with two beautiful billabongs nearby that contained all the food required for comfortable existence. File snakes, other reptiles, the longneck turtle, lily roots, aquatic birds and land animals that came to water were fair game.

The billabongs are *Ulñyunduboo* and *Kurriyul,* or as sometimes referred to by Europeans as the 'twin sister's' billabong are the names of Jack's mother and aunty. These can be identified on the maps of the Northern Territory in the area called Que Noy Gardens, Hang Gong's Lagoon and Pipe Billabong. The Dingle Darra Dingle Dung road is the black soil plain on the wagon track running between Old Bynoe Road and the mining fields in that area, taking in the Lucy Claim. The name Dingle Dara Dingle Dung was the name given by the McGinness children to the ore crusher machine which gave out that particular metallic sound when in use. The name was later transferred to the wagon track and remains as a fond reminder to the McGinness family of the place where the machine bogged and remained never to be removed until very recently.

Jungung

Abandoned steam machinery which belonged to the McGuinness family. Located near Darwin River, near old Southport Road. (Date: Unknown).
(Unknown, NTL, F. G. Franklin Collection, PH0109-0019).

Family Unit

Murrunduh (Frank)	*Ulñyunduboo* (Lucy McGinness)	Stephen Joseph McGinness	*Wultjur* (Charlie)	*Kurrmandum* (Mary-Ann)

Bernard Steven (*Murunda*)	John Francis (Michael, baptismal saints' name.) [*Kingulawiy*]	Margaret Cecilia [*Kurrmandum*]	Valentine Bynoe [*Wooddiwitch*]	Joseph Daniel [*Pumeri*]

All the McGinness children held *Koongurrukuñ* names because of *Ulñyunduboo* as well as English ones after the Saints.

Life at the Lucy Mine

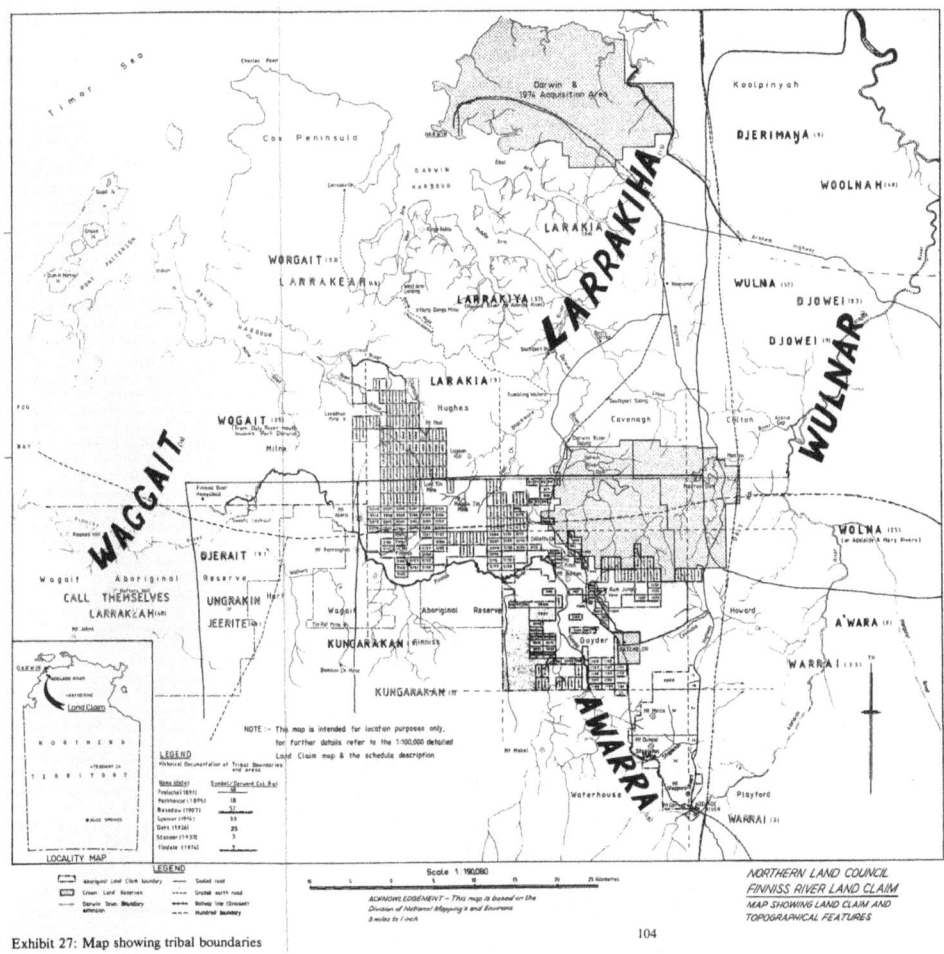

Map of the Finniss River Land Claim area showing the tribal boundaries. *Finniss River Land Claim*, exhibit 27, 104.

Happy times on country

To understand my father Jack's life it is important to mention the diversity of his early upbringing and to understand the complexity in the cultural fabric of life and the sad changes that happened in order for this history to unfold.

The land around *Mudgidirbirr* is closely associated with the area that provides the knowledge crucial to Jack's cultural responsibility, to his Aboriginal law and bordering country. *Kingulawuy* is a special area north of the Reynolds River. The name is shared with other people whose place is on the south side of the river and who had cultural connections to *Koongurrukuñ*. The land area is adjacent to *Koongurrukuñ* land to the north/northwest and the southern border of *Koongurrukuñ* land.

Jack shared the name *Kingulawiy* with the father of *Minnawooli* and his sister *Kurriyul*. The names *Kingulawiy, Minnawooli* and *Kurriyul* remain in the Jack McGinness family and the other surviving family of *Minnawooli* living at the Bagot Community in Darwin. Jack's aunty *Kurriyul Maranda'* wife and mother of *Moongee* shared the name with the daughter of *Kingulawiy*. Barney and Joe's names are also associated with the same area. Names signify responsibility associated to land and the social order effecting *Koongurrukuñ* People.

Land association is basic to Aboriginal people even through the people who were removed from tribal lands, the landscape is reflected in the names of the people. Other family groups with strong cultural ties to the McGinness families who relate to that cultural landscape live in Darwin. Those ties remain strong and are kept with the families' representative of their respective cultural landscape.

Koongurrukuñ remember *Larrakia, Wujikan, Wari* and *Nanggumerri* people who are in *Mungung* allegiance relationship with each other. These people are direct neighbours - *Larrakia* to the north, *Nanggumerri* to the south. *Wari* to the east and *Wajikan* to the west.

Other neighbours include *Minitjah* in the northeast and *Palamarinyan* in the southwest. *Palamarinyan* were referred to as the coastal *Koongurrukuñ* or *Pongoh Pongoh* people who spoke *Koongurrukuñ* dialect. Trade, ceremony, marriage and language links were vital components of the relationship.

Mining Interest on country

The people of the small communities who lived and worked the surrounding area of *Mudgidirbirr* were industrious. They fossicked and mined for tin, gold and tantalite. It is said that they enjoyed the fruits of their labor whenever they were able to produce an acceptable quota and be paid for the shipment. Those around *Mudgidirbirr* were mainly *Koongurrukuñ, MulukMuluk, Nangomerri, Dutjurrutj*, English, European, Irish and various others who happened to drop in. This tiny League of Nations worked together having a common interest and goal. They were all prospectors engaged in the early development of the mining industry in North Australia. The McGinness family was recognised as the primary people of the land that *Murrunduh* was head of the *Koongurrukuñ* and his sister *Ulñyunduboo* as Stephen McGinness's wife.

Other miners were Bert Smitherem and Jack Hopper, father of Jack Hopper son of *Kroormundum* who was separated from the McGinness family. Aboriginal people were heavily involved as miners and those who worked at *Mudgidirbirr* were Solomon *Taeboong Boong* who was known as Charlie Edwards because he both worked, and in a sense was adopted by, Harry Edwards. *Mooradoop, Dot Kumudom, Minna* and *Mickey Noongoonjool* were, parents of *Abluk* (also known as George Snape) and sister *Bessie Luniyook*. *Mickey Murinj* and *Minna* later came into Darwin and worked for Harry and Margaret Edwards.[3] *Minna* had a brother whose name was *Mongu* (also known as *Work WorkMuh*). *Chugoodah* and *Murrundah* their uncle's, both worked in the mines and accompanied the McGinness children everywhere they went. As the children's personal protectors *Chugoodah* and *Murrundah* they would take them to catch the train to go to Darwin to do their Easter duties of the Catholic Church or other important events. In high water time they would carry Margaret on their shoulders and the McGinness children had great affection for these family members. Joe later claimed that whereever he travelled, *Taeboong-boong* would make his presence known. Joe marvelled at this and said it was uncanny. Many myths and legends grew out of the region. One of the stories was about Ah Bo, a Chinese gardener, who it is said murdered *Jununapet*, his Aboriginal wife, and disposed of her body in one of the billabongs there. There remain other fascinating stories about this era - some quite intriguing.

Tis a Braw BrichtMoonlichtnichttaenicht

Life at the Lucy had its romantic as well as its serious and fun times. Jack's family stories of rousty nights when the rum was flowing, the competitive jesting that ensued around those get-togethers, and how small saplings were engaged in tossing the caber. Foot races, standing broad jump and other sports, plus the bar room antics that could be done out bush with the children joining in at times. This laid the foundations for the sporting prowess of the McGinness children later in life.

It is assumed, and there is little doubt, that Stephen wrote the penned verse below being the character he was, straight shooter, larrikin, political activist, entertainer and hard worker.

> Stephen McGinness came in from the Finniss
> With a cheque of a hundred and three
> He went down the town and acted the clown
> And finally got on the spree
> It was Stephen McGinness who came back to the Finniss
> His tail firmly tucked twixt his knees
> He could not bear the shout -
> So his fun soon ran out
> Like his cheque of a hundred and three
> [Joe McGinness often recited this verse throughout his life.]

---

3   Gilbert Henry 'Harry' Edwards married Margaret McGinness on the 27th August 1918, Jong, Siausa., NT Births, Deaths & Marriage, telephone conversation, 15 May 2019.

I never met my grandfather but this period was foundational for all the family and set their character where values were strongly imbued. My impression of grandfather, developed in later life, was that of a multifaceted man. Like my grandfather I believe that the world could be a better place if we emphasised 'values' more. The stories of the family continually reinforce these values.

Mining at the Lucy was dangerous. Jack told the story about the time Barney fell down the mine shaft and was pinned under one of the uprights and was calling for help. Val ran back to Mac and said 'Barney's down the mine and he's swearing.' Stephen asked what it was that Barney was saying and he was told 'Jesus Christ, it's heavy.' Totally strict about the use of bad language and blasphemy being a mortal sin, Stephen went down to deal with the matter. Getting to the surface he said, 'A man should give you the father of a hiding.' Barney, quite shaken, could not understand why he was going to be punished and he asked 'What for'? When told that he was swearing Barney was quick to defend himself saying that he was saying his prayers in case he was going to die. 'What might that be Barney?' asked Stephen. Barney's reply, 'I was saying Jesus, Joseph and Mary assist me.' With that he was spared the dreaded strop, which was referred to as the persuader.[4]

Mudgidirbirr Folk Stories

Other powers of persuasion were the legendry tales of *Koodooks*, the spiritual custodians of the land and in particular the ever present and watchful *Chingurruks* Aboriginal spiritual medicine men. These spirits were ever-present and watchful should anyone be disobedient and the *Koodooks* would catch you and play tricks on you or abandon you and as a result you may come to harm. The spirits were the disciplinarians of the land according to *Koongurrukuñ* folk law. *Buggleboar* and Boogyman were counterpart of Irish folk lore. *Quillulick,* the curlew, was the physical being of *Koongurrukuñ* mythology that was feared by people. Whenever the curlew calls it is a reminder to take good care and protect the children. The cultural story relates to the estranged mother in search of her child that had been separated from her for disciplinary reasons. The screech of the Curlew as the abductor of neglected children was the reminder to those who might not take their responsibility seriously.

The sound the children were most fearful of was *Bloongbloong,* a character developed at *Mudgidirbirr*. *Bloongbloong* was actually the childish imitation of the emu which made a deep throated sound. The children would lose no time in hopping into bed and covering their heads and going to sleep whenever they heard the call *"Bloongbloong".* In fact, it was a shadow image of a mythical creature

---

4   *NTTG*, 30 November 1918. It is not clear if this article is the same event referred to in the story but it confirms the dangers of mining at the Lucy.

portrayed by light against the canvas backdrop of the tent, a very frightening experience and larger than life puppet show. The shadow figure was someone cloaked with a felt hat strapped to a broom handle which bobbed up and down and would turn at the appropriate time as though looking towards them.

Stephen's Irish Reminiscence

Stephen would reminisce in patriotism of his beloved distant homeland and the family he left behind. He would tell stories and sing folk songs that he taught to his little family about his own upbringing and the land that was his heritage and birth right. He told them of his family of thirteen and that one of his sisters died from a broken back. Sadly, her death was caused when one of her brothers accidentally jumped on her while playing. Stephen was born on a British ship in New York Harbour on route to a new destination which meant he was a British subject. Stephen was later drafted into the Merchant Navy.

During his pensive moments he would sing;

> Roamin' in the gloamin'
> On the bonny Banks of Clyde
> Roamin' in the gloamin'
> With a lassie by my side
> When the sun has gone to rest
> That's the time that I love best
> Always lovely roamin' in the gloamin.
> ['We sang that over and over with Dad.']

With that *Ulñyunduboo* would join in and dance the Irish Jig taught to her by Stephen. It was jovial to hear her sing the Irish ditties and do the highland fling and how she would join Stephen when he sang

Tis a brawbrichtmoonlichtnichttaenitcht (It's a good bright moonlight night tonight).[5]

> My old woman went to Scotland for a holiday
> She's got Scotland on the brain, She's drivin me insane
> She used to give eggs and bacon for my breakfast once
> But now it's nothing else but porridge, now for months and months
> She does like a little bit of Scotch ye kin, she does like a little bit of Scotch

---

5   Special thanks to Ros Angeles and Annette Bethel who provided the correct spelling.

Jungung

> In the middle of the night she begins to sing
> Jumps out of bed with a highland fling
> She christened me Sandy her ways you ought to watch
> With a brawbrichtmoonlicht night taenicht
> She does like a little bit of scotch ye ken
> She does like a little bit of scotch ho ho
> She does like a little bit of scotch

The McGinness children all sang the songs their father taught them and made up their own brand of nursery rhymes with their mother's help. They composed a song about a turtle they kept as a pet. Its fate was to be eaten when it was big enough, but they became so attached it eventually died of natural causes.

Family Songs
This piece could be sung as a round.   /   Translation

The old *Koo gorrngol*
The old *koogorrngoll*
A very funny fellow is the old *Koo gorrngol*l
We got him when he was a *Numinjuk*
And now he's big as a *Ngurrtt*

Translation

The old long neck turtle
The old long neck turle
A very funny fellow is the old long neck turtle
We got him when he was a small turtle and
Now he is as big and fat as a short neck turtle

A lullaby *Ulñyunduboo's* rendition sang similar to the tune of "Goosie Goosie Gander"

NgorrNgorrWuwuknumi   (sleep children)
KootrumumKoortumun
Koomuleegujurruh
Toot tah mu Jorrdud
Ngin in yuh
wurruhwurruh
Kain Kaingoh
Kairnkairngoh

Life at the Lucy Mine

A song relating to special cultural places

KoorruwukLookurrurkin

MukudahMukudah
KooluwurriKooluh
Yirrkubindooluh
Yirrkuminyiminyiyulluh
Yirriyirribeyjuh
KuluhKuluhBeyjuha
YirriYirriBeyjuh
BorroongBorroonglok
Borroongborroonglok
NgunuNgunu la La
koori Mandai
WidjiWidjiBurroon
WdjjiWidjiBurroon   Ho!

A *Wooroomboot* is a hairy caterpillar with a very nasty sting. The sting is very painful and avoided by *Koongurrukuñ* and is part of the dangerous bush creatures. Whenever they were embarking on a hunting trip they used to chant "Don't pootum foot that *Wooroomboot*". Joe sang a ditty as a cure to combat the effects of being stung. The children all learnt how to apply his theory in other circumstances as a method to transfer the pain back to its source using this approach.

Nginyuguh Woorroomboot.	You are the *Woorroomboot*
Ngirrguh Joe	I am Joe
Nginyuguh Woorroomboot	I am the *Woorroomboot*
Nginyuguh Joe	You are Joe

Like the other adopted phrase 'It seems we might have to plait the grass!' the following phrase has been handed down to the present generation who may experience contentious or unsuitable situations quote; 'Don't pootim foot that *Woorroomboot.*'

Music was very much part of life at *Mudgidirbirr*. Singing lullabies became a tradition in Jack's family, songs from *Mudgidirbirr* would be sung to his children and later accompanied by his wife-to-be Violet Wakelin. Bedtime stories were perfect times for Jack on occasions to observe his obligations to his children as a Catholic. Jack would recite Hail Holy Queen, The Rosary and The Confite and we could join in when we wished. *Adeste Fideles and Oh Sulutarus* were hymns sung in Latin that the children loved to hear because they were sung in language much like the songs sung in *Koongurrukuñ*.

The children loved listening to the music even though Jack had no illusions about the tone of his voice and always said that his singing sounded like a goat walking over corrugated iron. Nevertheless, favourite melodies were *Lock Lomond, The Rose of Tralee* and other nonsense songs to sing the children to sleep.

When Father Papered the Parlor

When father papered the parlor
You couldn't see pa for paste
Dabbing it here, dabbing it there
There was paste and paper every where
Mother was stuck on the ceiling
The kids were stuck on the floor
I never saw such a bloomin' family so stuck up before.

Billie Boy [was a real family favourite']

Where have you been Billy boy my Billy Boy
Oh where have you been charming Billy
I have been to seek a wife, she's the the darlin' of "me" life
She's a young thing and cannot leave her mother
Can she bake a cherry pie Billy Boy my Billy Boy
Can she bake a cherry pie charming Billy
She can bake a cherry pie quick as a cat can wink his eye
She's a young thing and cannot leave her mother
Oh how old is she Billy Boy my Billy Boy
Oh how old is she charming Billy
She is six times seven twenty-eight and eleven
She's a young thing and cannot leave her mother

In later years Violet added to the repertoire her favorites "The Old Kentucky Home" and "Pretty Red Wings" Her favorite being,

Prairie Moon

Roll along prairie moon, roll along while I croon
Swinging high in the sky prairie moon
Way up there in the blue maybe you're lonely too
Shine above lamp of love prairie moon
I need your tender light to make things bright
You know I'm so alone tonight
Far away shed your beams on the girl of my dreams
Tell her too I've been true prairie moon

The End of an era

Stephen McGinness died on the 26th October 1918.[6] He died in the Darwin Hospital from complications arising from gangrene. Unfortunately details of the original accident that resulted in the onset of gangrene are not known.

Darwin: Forced Separation/Assimilation Policy

After Stephen McGinness' death his children were subject to Government legislation for the removal of Half-caste children from tribe and country. The process proved to be catastrophic for those who were removed. The action not only caused permanent harm to the social fabric of Aboriginal society it threatened their passage forward in assuming their cultural rights within their tribe. It interfered with their social status and proof of identity as Indigenous people of their country, severely affecting and threatening their very existence.

The forced removal of the McGinness family from *Mudgidirbirr* and their lost contact with their family interrupted their progress in tribal obligation that was vital for them as young *Koongurrukuñ* people at a most important development stage of their lives in terms of social and cultural status. It is fortunate though that through their mother's insistence on being close to them and finding employment in and around Kahlin compound meant that their separation from their land and people was temporary.

The Government policies designed to stop multicultural marriages resulted in many White men abandoning their Aboriginal children and playing no role in their upbringing. Despite these policies Stephen McGinness cared for his family

---

6   *NT Times & Gazette (NTTG)*, 26 October 1918.

deeply and did all he could to ensure their wellbeing. He also instilled a sense of family responsibility in to other White men with Aboriginal families to ensure they put children into safe responsible homes.

Family and Cultural Connection

Up until the removal from their family the McGinness children had no knowledge of other direct family descendants issuing from the younger members *Wultjur* and *Koorrmundum* except for a daughter born to Dot *Kumandum* who died in infancy

The McGinness family remembered Jack Hopper half-caste son of *Kroomundum* and Jack Hopper senior a white fettler and Jack's Hopper brother, *Leewooringoo* Tommy whose father was *Chingoonook* Ned. They were able to trace little Jack Hopper's whereabouts only as far as when he was taken in to live with the Wilson family in Darwin. They often wondered what became of little Jack Hopper. Their other cousin Frank *Moongi*, son of *Kurriyul*, and their uncle Frank *Maranda* born 1918, did survive and they did enjoy limited contact with the McGinness's. McGinness oral history tells that *Kurriyul*, *Moongi's* mother later lived with Old Andy Snape, a European man who came with his family to *Mudgidirbirr*. As a result of his mother having lived with Old Andy Snape *Moongi* adopted the surname Snape.

The last time Jack McGinness saw Frank *Moongi* was in the late fifties when Frank was at East Arm settlement and Jack was working there. George Abluk (Havlock) born 1922, son of *Noongoonjool* a *MulukMuluk* man guardian with the responsibility to keep *Koongurrukuñ* knowledge, was also known as George Snape. *Noongoonjool's* registered date of birth was 1900 making him the same age as Barney McGuinness.

Name bestowal is of significant importance in Aboriginal custom for the purpose of retaining responsibility to land and cultural survival. The brothers, Charlie and Andy Snape, have names that relate to country along with the McGinness men knowing their tribal connection to *Koongurrukuñ* people.

Moongi and other relatives lived and worked around *Mudgidirbirr* up until the untimely death of Stephen McGinness. Members and descendants of the families from *Mudgidirbirr* continue to recognise their connection to each other.

Naming ceremonies called *ngirrwut* are important cultural obligations that happen at important events such as bogey, (*Tjaluk*) or burial ceremonies. *ngirrwut* is the process of transferring names that requires responsibility and obligation. The *ngirrwut* for the Jack McGinness family took place in 1967 at *Lok Lanji, Darwin River*. *Tjaluk* is the *Koongurrukuñ* word used for the practice in mortuary rites (washing/cleansing) while more recently a bogey was held at *Mudgidirbirr* in 2005 following the passing of the youngest of the McGinness family, Joe McGinness and was attended by representatives from each of the five McGuinness / McGinness family groups.

Robert Mills, ceremony on country for Joe McGinness, c2003.
(Unknown, Mills Collection).

Jungung

Wetji bogey, ceremony on country c1963. *Quinung* (Daisy) dancing front left, Ruby Shepherd and Albert Ah Loy in foreground, Middle background Tony and Kate Bishop (children) (Unknown, Lockwood, Collection).

Land People Association

The Secretary family connect to the McGinness family through their father *Kibangbung* and mother *Barrin-ginj/Danyinil* who were the parents of Bobby *Gwil-murinji, Topsy-Tjuani* and Gabriel-*Bulainjoonj*.

McGinness history has it that Frank Secretary, known as King George, was kinsman to *Murrunduh* and *Ulñyunduboo*. Like their land these people are in *Munggung* relationship to the McGinness family, which Jack was sure to point out to his family. The word *Munggung* is more commonly known as cousin or *Bunji*.

According to Val McGinness, Frank had a good reputation as a very capable worker / assistant and was respected by his charge Mr Adams, who was the editor of the Government *Times and Gazette,* and the other staff members.[7] He also thought that perhaps Mr Adams may have referred to Frank as his secretary, hence the name. Usage of names given to Aborigines by their employers was common at that time. Some names however were quite unacceptable and distasteful as can be identified in other books and accounts.

Jack Hanson was the linotype operator at the *Northern Territory Times and Gazette.* The linotype machine looked like a huge typewriter and its head needed to be primed with methylated spirits to operate it.[8] The newspaper office was situated opposite the Church of England Church and the Court House was next door on the Esplanade. The newspaper office later became the health centre when *The Times* office relocated to Smith Street.

The Town Hall was situated opposite Brown's Mart. When the McGinness family went to the Don Pictures in Cavenagh Street they took pride in the opening display on the screen that featured the word *Larrakia* with a coastal view from the Court House looking towards Channel Island. They could see *Koongurrukuñ* country on the other side of the harbor. Val said that its purpose was to attract the interest of overseas visitors. This would have to be the first public form of advertising at the beginning of tourism for the Territory.

There was a large generator at the back and Mr Wittle was the council worker whose job as the lamplighter was to see that the lights were switched off at the generator.

The new beginning: fighter and campaigner for equal rights
A Political Minefield

Stephen McGinness was always aware of the existing political situation and the predicament in which his children were placed. Coming from the 'old country', as it was called, Stephen knew the political situation with his background of The Orange and The Green and the consequences of loss of identity through immigration. His children were classified illegitimate, Half-Caste and were subjects under the *Native Affairs Act.* Aborigines were not entitled to own property and Stephen's objection to the Government can be noted in his own political stance when he registered the three mines in the Bynoe Harbour area as recorded Maranda, Maggie and Lucy. He named the claims using his family members Lucy after his wife *Maranda* her brother and Maggie, Stephen's and *Ulñyunduboo's* daughter (Margaret).

---

7   Adams, Albert William was a partner in a successful newsagency in Cavenagh Street during this period. For further details see Farram, *Charles James Kirkland.*
8   Hansen, John Joseph, For further details see Farram, *Charles James Kirkland.*

Jungung

He was adamant his children should learn to read and write and took it upon himself to teach them at night using kerosene, carbide lamps or candle light. When Barney started working he had the reputation that the log books and time sheets were among the best kept records as he wrote in fine copperplate hand writing. Although they only had two years of formal education through the convent, their continued desire to learn was evident in the things Jack and his family, Margaret and brothers Barney, Joe and Valentine aspired to.

Stephen's death in 1918 had drastic consequences for the family, particularly for Jack when he was approaching 'young man' status in his own country. It was a bad time to be removed from kin and country to be under and subject to the protection policy of the Government of Australia. Jack's whole world took yet another turn when he was forced to relocate to live in Darwin and begin a new life in an unfamiliar community under a new regime and social order. This virtually ended his tribal life as a *Koongurrukuñ t*ribesman to become a warrior in an alien environment in someone else's country: Darwin. Dispossession and denial of freedom of movement subsequently lead to his taking up the fight for justice and equal rights.

Family on country [Lucy Claim] L-R: Speedy, Joyce, Mim, Kathy, Vi. Joan, Aunty Maggie, Sadie, Brian - Jack's 'Challuk', 1973. (Unknown, Mills Collection).

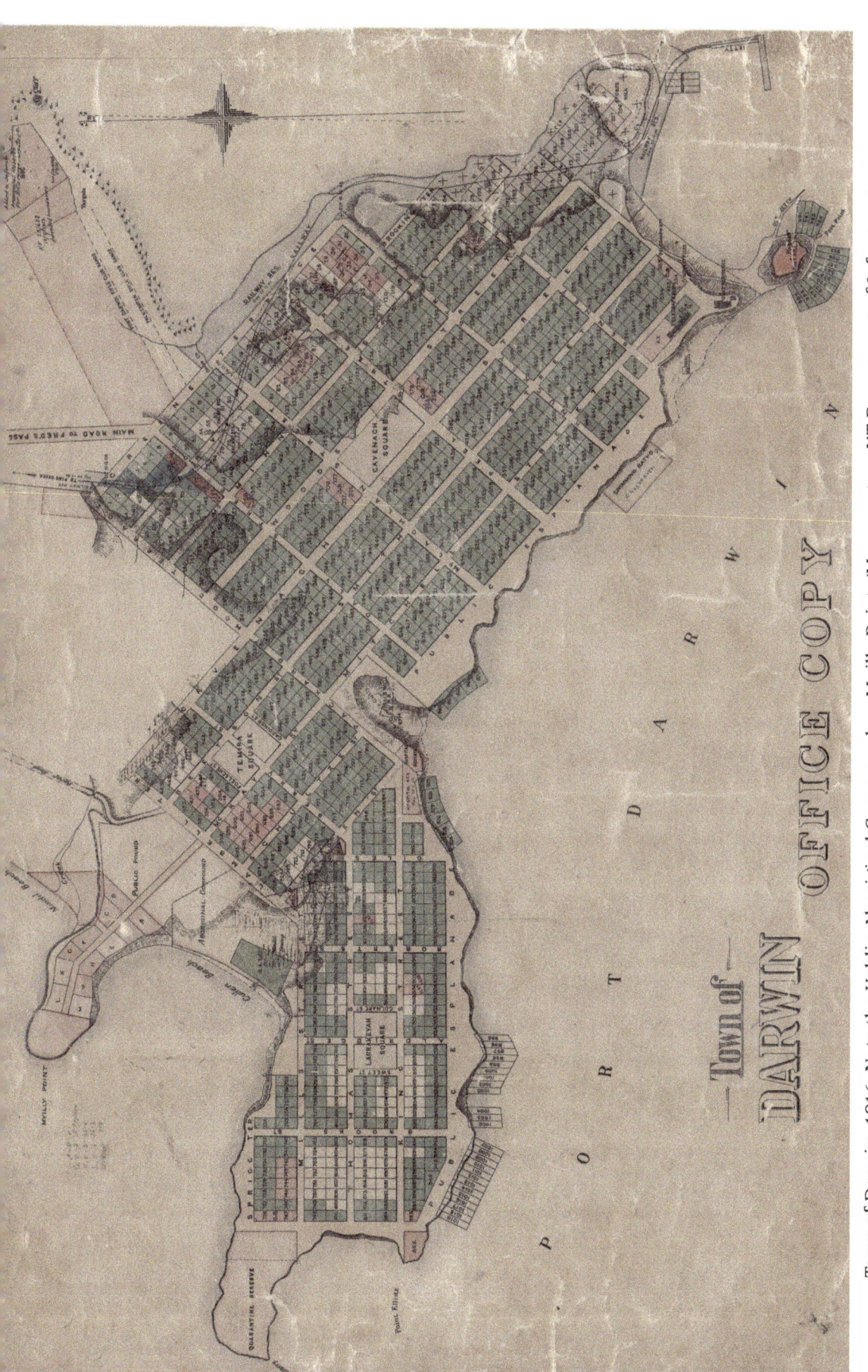

Town of Darwin, 1916. Note the Kahlin Aboriginal Compound on Myilly Point. (Map courtesy NT Department of Infrastructure, Planning and Logistics © Northern Territory of Australia.)

Chapter 4:
A New Life in Darwin During the 1920s

This section of the story takes readers on a journey through a period when the Northern Territory was developing its own identity as a significant section of the Australian Government. This was when Darwin was beginning to develop as a northern port and vital link with southern ports through Asia and eventually the world. It tells about developing relationships between different races and how they became stretched to breaking point due to the harsh environs of a settlement in the making plus Government policies that were unjust, divisive and racially discriminating.

This is the story of a man who took what was regarded as "The plight of the Aborigine" to the people of Australia and the Government and did not relent until he won the recognition that inequality and social injustice existed between Aboriginal and non-Aboriginal people. Jack was forced to live in Darwin subject to the *Aboriginal Ordinance* which automatically declared him a "Ward of the State" subject to the *Native Affairs Act*. Under this legislation Aboriginal people were rounded up and kept in bondage for decades. Compounds, settlements, reserves and missions were being developed to hold the "full-blood Aboriginal" people and the fast-growing population of "part Aboriginal" children.

The Government believed that the threat of insufficient funding and supplies to adequately cater for Aboriginal people and the need to prevent exploitation made it necessary to control them by restricting their movements and living arrangements. A section of land overlooking Myilly Point was fenced off as a holding reserve and a compound behind where the Police horse paddocks and goat yard were situated. The Compound was called Kahlin and became the clearing house from where the children of mixed descent were removed to missions that had been set up on Goulburn Island, Croker Island, Bathurst Island and the Emerald River Mission on Groote Eylandt.

Children of mixed descent were taken from their Aboriginal mothers and distributed to the various religious denominations to remain under their complete control. Reserves and later, settlements were established for "Full Blood Aborigines" at Bagot Reserve a few miles further out from the Port of Darwin. The terms "Full Blood" and "Half-caste" distinguished between the original Native people and children who were born of the union between Aboriginal women and the non-Aboriginal men. Jack was subjected to this system after the death of his Irish father and his family's subsequent removal from their homeland, separated from their "Full Blood" mother under *'The Act'*. The two youngest boys were taken with their mother to Kahlin Compound in Darwin but *Ulñyunduboo* was placed in the fenced off section behind the compound which held "Full Blood Natives". Valentine and Joseph were separated from *Ulñyunduboo* at the ages of 3 and 5. Jack and Barney were directed to go to the convent on insistence of the Mother Superior who had pledged her loyalty to Stephen that the Catholic Church would protect them from the authorities. They were there only a short period deemed as being too old for the student population, so they were eventually moved to Kahlin Compound. This was the first time in their lives that the McGinness children were classified as being different to the rest of the community and their first experience of cold hard racism. At this time Jack was sent to a training programme in Delissaville.

Ulñyunduboo in her 'House Girl' uniform, c1920s. Oral testimony says she worked for Doctor Fothergill. (Unknown, Mills Collection).

> "(from Kathy Mills)...Well, she, of course, she wanted to be with her children, her babies. They were only infants.
>
> So the story is, she begged the authorities to take her in as a worker, and she worked in the Kahlin Compound laundry so she could be close to her two babies that were in the half-caste [compound].
>
> But she, herself, stayed in the black quarters. You know, it was chained off—it was separated by a fence—the blacks were behind the fence of the half-caste compound."

Young men who were considered old enough to work were placed in employment as laborers and domestic workers or transported across the harbour to the newly established training colony at Delissaville. There, the young men were put to work as gardeners, fence builders and caring for stock. A salary scale was set for each participant and they were told that the accrued amount would be available when they left the colony.[9]

Jack's first years of separation were spent at Delissaville. However on his departure he did not receive any of his accrued wages. Reflecting on this, Jack said he would not beg for what was his and that he would put it down to experience. Restrictions were in place for Half-castes who wished to operate outside The Compound precinct and Jack was told that he had to apply for a Certificate of Exemption for this to happen. The exemption certificate was issued to those who could meet and agree to the conditions that applied by the Superintendent of The Compound or the Chief Protector of Aborigines. One of those conditions stated that the person was required to forfeit their identity as an Aborigine under *The Act* to become free to operate outside the jurisdiction of The Compound. For some it seemed to be an alternative and a means of escape from control of the system. However, the exemption was not permanent and could be revoked at the discretion of any authoritative body or representative.

When Jack was old enough he refused to apply for exemption on the grounds that his father was a British Subject and therefore he should not be forced to apply for an exemption. He claimed that he should be free to follow his own ambition. His argument was ignored and he was treated as an absconder, renegade and trouble maker. Jack set about looking for work and eventually found work with his brother-in-law Harry Edwards who was by this time married to his sister Margaret. Harry Edwards ran a contracting business based at his premises in Wood Street. It was here that Jack came to be taught the trades of wheelwright and coopering.

---

9 'Stolen Wages' is a common story to Aboriginal people throughout Australia. Many are still seeking compensation from state and federal Governments.

Jack claimed he was denied his natural birth rights as a son of Stephen McGinness who was a British subject, and enslaved as a 'Ward of the State' under the *Native Affairs Act 1910* because his mother was a 'full-blood native' of Australia. He never accepted the conditions of *The Act* and condemned its practices as unjust, and set his sights on removing those oppressive shackles.

The removal of children and the possibility of adverse effects which might threaten or cause insecurity was not a Government or religious priority nor was it considered to be of any great consequence by those who administered *The Act*. Jack remained conscious of his personal experience and claimed that he had been dispossessed of his inherent rights; his birthright as the son of a British Subject to be recognised as such was denied and his birthright and status as a *Koongurrukuñ* son of his mother who was a 'full blood native' meant he was denied and dispossessed of his entire human rights as being of any consequence what so ever. Jack felt these injustices keenly throughout his life. It was a repeated family story and an illustration of the cycle of dispossession. Stephen McGinness was trying to prevent his family from experiencing the dispossession of rights that he had experienced.

> Such was Jack's "Inherent Status" through dispossession of land
>
> Loss of natural family through isolation from land and environment
>
> Loss of language through separation from family elders
>
> Loss of cultural practice through disorientation and foreign influences
>
> Loss of recognition and power through denial of hierarchical structure and heirs apparent

This was fire in the belly stuff for Jack and he set about changing ways of thinking and pursuing human rights for all Aboriginal people wherever he could and by any means available to him. Jack had in fact anticipated the findings of the 'Bring Them Home Report' released in 1997. He was a visionary in the sense that he identified and acknowledged this dispossession in the 1920s.[10]

Sadly, Jack died before the Federal Government heard the compensation and reparation claims made by the Stolen Generation Corporation highlighting the loss of identity through removal and dispossession that consequentially caused disadvantage to the people who were removed. Removal and dispossession

---

10   Kathy Mills has been part of three Royal Commissions examining injustices identified and experience by her father in the 1920s and 1930s.

echoed Jack's earlier claims of a loss of inheritance, identity and lost history. The consequence of those factors is obvious today and stands as a tragic reminder for descendants of the Stolen Generations. The reality is that descendants of the Stolen Generation are now referred to as the 'Lost Generation', ramifications of which induce family and community dysfunction. Far too many children suffered as a result of separation from their families, country and culture, they are the casualties to this present age. Vital cultural and family information continue to elude them adding to the dilemma faced by many of the Stolen Generation and their descendants. Advice by their legal team at that time of legal preparations discouraged any claims of genocide by the Stolen Generations based on the claims process itself as well as legal requirement necessary to proceed.

Harry Edwards and Jack McGinness at the Edwards home on Wood Street, Darwin, c1920s. (Unknown, Mills Collection.)

A New Life in Darwin During the 1920s

Official contingent of A.I.F. departed Darwin on SS 'Changsha' on 26 April 1915. Names and Nos.: Allen, Charles Ernest,1033; Bowman, Adam, 1034; Buckley, Jeremiah, 1517; Butters (aka Buttercase); Robert Dingwall, 1376; Dick, Samuel Henry, 1036; Downing, Llewellyn Selwyn, 1037; **Edwards, Gilbert Henry (Harry)**, 1038; Every, Gilbert, 1039; Fawcett, James Edward, 1040; Garr,William, 3051; Giles, Leslie Henry, 1044; Godfrey, John Stewart, 1042; Gracie (aka Herring), Frank Valentine, 1041; Greenshields, John Hamilton, 1042; Gregory, S.A., - ; Levy, Lerner Vivian, 1045; Lewis, Robert James,Capt; McNeil, James, 1048; Meredith, Frederick Richard, 1047; Morrison, Alfred P.,- ; Parkhouse Victor Roy, 7361; Pott, Harry Bunce, 1051; Rogers, Cyril Stewart, 1052; Stiles, William, 1053; Termansen, Frank, 1064; Xuereb, Anthony, 1055.
(Unknown, NTL, Jean A. Austin Collection, PH0412-0183).

Gilbert Henry 'Harry' Langdon Edwards, a Gallipoli veteran of World War 1, brother-in-law, tutor, friend and stalwart played a very significant role in supporting Jack and his brothers' lives during the 1920s following the death of Stephen McGinness. Harry Edwards, born in Tasmania in June 1873, first came into contact with Stephen McGinness in the period of the Lucy Mine.[11]

Harry challenged the unfair treatment of Aboriginal people, speaking personally and with authority, being closely associated through his marriage to Jack's sister

---
11 Edwards, Gilbert Henry Langdon, Attestation papers 1915.

Margaret.[12] Harry had also pledged his loyalty to Stephen McGinness on his death-bed, as did the Catholic Mother Superior, to care for Stephen's children and protect them from the clutches of the authorities. While in hospital upon hearing what had happened on their removal from the land, Stephen McGinness's instructions to Harry were to 'blow the place [The Lucy Mine] to smithereens.'[13]

Harry Edwards had government approval under the *Aboriginal Ordinance* to take the McGinness boys on as apprentices. Jack was in his employ when Harry went south to Melbourne in the early 1920s. Valentine and Barney were working for Dr Cook at the hospital in Packard Street. Barney was the first medical assistant to Dr Cook and Valentine drove the ambulance as well as doubling as a courier driver.[14]

Harry Edwards was a hard task master, had he not been so, then things might not have turned out as they did. Jack acknowledged Harry's dedication to foster the younger McGinness boys, teaching them the occupation of blacksmithing, wheelwright and sinking wells around Darwin. Harry never stopped promoting fair treatment and respect for Aboriginal people while remaining loyal to his promise to Steven McGinness.

Harry had a house in Wood Street where he carried out his contracting business and where he kept his family and passed on his knowledge to his apprentices. He was intolerant of any form of discrimination or racism. Harry respected and expected equality and according to Jack and Margaret he was known to fiercely demonstrate his objections wherever it was an obvious concern. One such incident related was when a man on meeting the couple said, 'How you going Maggie?' Harry took great umbrage to his flamboyant approach and told him in no uncertain terms, 'In future Sir, whenever you speak to my wife you will refer to her as Mrs Edwards, or you will have to prepare to defend yourself.' Val McGinness's version of the story stated that with that he knocked the fellow to the ground.

As well as being their brother-in-law, Harry Edwards was their tutor, mentor and champion of the cause. Not only did he teach them practical work skills but he endeavoured to promote through them a black sports club. He trained them in track and field sports, and the arts of pugilism and football. He promoted and encouraged them to take part in management and official coaching. Harry was to become their personal trainer and manager, but he would train any Aboriginal who wished to participate.

---

12 Gilbert Henry 'Harry' Langdon Edwards married Margaret McGinness on the 27th August 1918. Jong, Siausa., NT Registry of Births, Deaths & Marriage, telephone conversation, 15 May 2019.
13 Mills, K. Personal communication with Matthew Stephen, 24 May 2019.
14 Dr Cecil Cook was chief medical officer and chief protector of Aborigines in the Northern Territory from 1927 to 1939.

Joe McGinness competing in a high jump competition in Darwin, c 1920s. Joe broke the unofficial pre-war record at 6 foot 1inch. Barney McGinness stands in a white suit to the right. It is possible Barney was officiating the competition. (Unknown, Mills Collection).

The McGinness name was synonymous with Darwin sport from the 1920s to World War II. Collectively the four brothers participated in athletics, billiards, boxing, cycling, Australian rules football and soccer. They each had their own specialties and stories in sport.

Barney was the first Aboriginal Aussie rules central umpire and sports official in Darwin. His career as an umpire for Aussie rules football was not without incident, being repeatedly subjected to objections of a racial nature to his officiating games. His achievement has been played down and trivialised. Between 1922 and 1930 Barney participated in both Australian rules football and athletics. Between 1929 and 1941 Barney applied to register as a Northern Territory Football League central umpire nine times. He was rejected outright on four occasions and his opportunities severely limited due to the racism that existed in the football league during this pre World War II period. His single handed battle to umpire in Darwin during an era when Darwin football was riven by racial prejudice and bigotry is unprecedented. His struggle was at the centre of the umpiring disputes that saw the 1934-35 NTFL season end in acrimony with Waratahs forfeiting the Grand Final to Buffaloes. This was the catalyst to the split in the NTFL and the formation of the White only Darwin Football League during the 1935-36 season: in effect a Colour Bar. Despite the prejudice shown towards him. Barney loved football and continued to support the game after World War II.

Jungung

Valentine was the pre-war middleweight champion in boxing while Joe held the pre-war record for the high jump. Spurgeon Nicholls was the referee when Valentine fought Andy Wright to win by knockout in the 7th round. Val was supposed to go to Canberra to further his career, but that never eventuated. Jack was a fierce competitor in the broad jump and triple-jump but did not hold any title. Joe held the pre-war high jump title but was beaten by Sebastian Briston, Barney's stepson, by an inch only to be beaten by Tommy Cusack in 1952 at the Darwin Show. All records were unofficially recorded but recognised in the Aboriginal community. Reuben Cooper held the record for the sprint but his time has been lost or not been appropriately recorded. Jack's involvement and role in Australian rules football will be discussed later in this chapter.

Harry Edwards had good supporters and friends and two in particular, according to Val, were Victor Kuffiarnus and his brother-in-law Ferman Lareeki. Lareeki's wife Carmen and daughter Teresa became good friends with Margaret Edwards

Jack was involved in many of the social issues before he left the Territory to go to Melbourne for a short time with his sister Margaret and her husband Harry Edwards in the early 1920s. The main issues confronting Aboriginal people at this time were incarceration and inequality, and Aboriginal people and their supporters took action to call for the abolition of the exemption card. The Dog Tag, as it was called, was discriminatory and restricted the aspirations of Aboriginal people.

Joe McGinness

In 1934 Kahlin Compound was undergoing change and Valentine and Joe, with a few others, started to exert pressure on the establishment to improve the conditions effecting Aboriginal people under *The Act*. They knew that things weren't exactly as they should have been, but did not know how to go about changing the situation. They approached Xavier Herbert who was Superintendent of Kahlin Compound and he encouraged them to go ahead and demonstrate and stand up for their rights.[15] Joe McGinness said, 'Xavier Herbert more or less encouraged and supported our protests and helped us organise our action plan. We were all about 18 years of age and clearly unhappy with the treatment we were receiving at the hands of the Government.'

---

15   Xavier Herbert was Superintendent of Kahlin Compound 1935-1936.

These young men formed a delegation to present a log of claims to the Protector of Aborigines, Dr Cecil Cook and the Administrator Gilruth.[16] The claims highlighted the exemption card and a request to meet with the Parliamentary Standing Committee on these issues. The fathers of Half-caste children also sought to introduce a Bill under the name of Eurasian Australian League for the sole purpose of protecting the children of mixed race and giving them their own identity. The term Eurasian was tossed about but never endorsed and later The Half-caste Progressive Association was adopted.

The deputation gathered outside Government House and it was noted that Harold Nelson, the Northern Territory's only member of the Commonwealth House of Representatives at the time, was at government house when this action was taken.[17] The administration's response was to dismiss the delegation as 'Yella Fellas' making a fuss. It was also stated that a scuffle took place and the Chief of Police, Stretton, was hit with a *nulla nulla*.[18]

According to Joe McGinness, the protesting men involved included Ruben Cooper, Bill Muir, Robert Roman, Bob Shepard, Jim Scully. While not all highly educated these men knew that the treatment they were experiencing was not just. However, World War II was on the horizon and the group disbanded and some instead volunteered for enlistment into the Army to fight for their country and put their personal fight on hold.

Of these young men, Robert Shepard was a veteran of the First World War 1. Joe McGinness, Bill Muir and Robert Roman enlisted and served in battle overseas. Bill Muir and others were to become decorated soldiers as written in *Black Diggers* and *Son of Alyandubu*. [A list of Aboriginal servicemen from NT.]

After the war Joe got married and settled in Cairns, North Queensland. He became President of the FAACTSI freedom for rights movement in north Queensland and continued to address the issues he had started to raise with his mates in Kahlin Compound.[19] FAACTSI along with the national movement was very involved in bringing about the Referendum of 1967 and the "Yes" vote.

---

16 Although this anecdote relates to the mid 1930s when the Administrator was Lt Col Robert Hunter Weddell, Kathy refers to Gilruth. Similar to the many Captain Cook stories that abound in the Northern Territory Gilruth is often referred to as the Administrator prior to World War II in oral history testimony despite the fact that he left the Territory in 1919.
17 Harold Nelson, Northern Territory Member of the Lower house of Federal Parliament, 1922 to 1934.
18 A *nulla nulla* is a hardwood fighting stick.
19 The Federal Council for the Advancement of Aborigines and Torres Strait Islanders.

Jungung

NT Aboriginal Servicemen WWI to Vietnam[20]

Name	Service Number[21]
World War I	
Allen, Willie	50246
Carmody, Christopher	Q21137
Cummins, George	
Dare, Thomas	
Kelly, George	
Ludgate, Frank	
McKenzie, Alex	N74429
McKinnon, Alexander	2230
Prentice, Fredrick	2579
Shepherd, Robert	4445
Wallace, Daniel	4448
Havelett, Harry (real name Hablett,)	3498

Name	Service Number[21]
World War II	
Abala, Stephen (Son of Barney McGinness.)	DX 895
Abbott, Arnold	
Abbott, Gordon	D663
Alison, Alfie	
Ansell, Jack	DX968
Benson, Max	SX21771
Bingapoor, John	
Blackmore, Nugget	DX1001
Bray, Harry	DX960
Brumby, Jack	DX961
Butler, Richard 'Dick'	
Clarke, William	
Cleary, Cameron	
Conway, Alec	DX953
Conway, Mort	
Cooper, Jack	D665
Costello, Michael	
Croker, Jack	
Dempsey, Bill	
Dubois, Roy	SX21245
Fejo, Samuel	D11
Hampton, Noel	154552
Hampton, Walter	SX1669
Hayes, Phillip	SX11564
Hughes, John	
Kennedy, Dannama	SX16558
Khan, Rocky	
King, George	
Kruger, Alec	D634
Laughton, Fredrick	
Laughton, Herbert	S77416
Laughton, Mick	D612
Liddle, Harold	SX12489
Liddle, Milton	SX28057
Lowe, Alexander	SX30670
Martin, Ted	
McDonald, Alec	
McGinness, Joseph 'Joe'	DX 977
McLennan, William	51616/D12
McMasters, Albert	DX954
Muggleton, Fredrick	
Muir, William 'Billy'	
Neale, John	

---

20 List compiled from Bray, Laughton, & Foster, *Aboriginal Ex-Servicemen of Central Australia*, 1-3. & Cramp, *Worth Fighting For*.

21 If service number not in publication an NAA record search was undertaken. Service numbers identified from place of birth in the Northern Territory and/or place of enlistment in the Northern Territory.

Name	Service Number[21]
Odegaard, Leo	DX996
Reid, Charles	
Roman, Robert	
Ross, Henry	
Schaber, Billy	
Schaber, Jack	
Schaber, Roy	SX19103
Scully, William	DX 945
Smith, Frank	
Smith, Jim	
Smythe, Clement	SX31212
Smythe, Lindsay	
Stirling, Paddy	D627
Stokes, Donald	DX971
Taylor, Alex	140782
Tilmouth, Roy	DX951
Turner, Alex	
Walkington, Ben	QX41650

Korean War	
Butler, Arthur	
Hampton, Reginald	
Laughton, Alan	

Malaya	
Dubois, Clive	
Shaw, Geoff	

Name	Service Number[21]
Vietnam War	
Briscoe, William	
Espey, Linton	
Goddard, Thomas	
Cubillo, Steve	710091
Laughton, Kenny	
Markam, Michael	4719525
Mayo, Desmond	4717744
Miller, David	
Muir, Alan	4721888
Tilmouth, Charles	
Tilmouth, Richard	
White, Brian	

Peace Time Service in Australia	
Ambrose, William	
Forrester, Vincent	
Hampton, Eric	
Hampton, Roy	
O'Callaghan, Anthony	
Parke, Lance	
Presley, Alfred	

Jungung

Jack always regretted that he had never enlisted, stating that he was too young for the First World War and too old for the Second World War, but he instead worked for Manpower on the railway in Katherine during the war period. The Manpower Directorate was formed in 1942 by the Federal Government to ensure labour was mobilised in strategic industries.

Richard 'Dick' Butler & Valentine McGinness, c 1920s. Dick enlisted in the Second AIF in 1939. He was accepted into Australia's permanent military forces in 1946. He retired from the Army in 1961. (Unknown, Mills Collection).

Valentine McGinness

Valentine recalled that life in Darwin was far from being dull and besides the political fracas there were good times that became legendary family tales. One story centres around a car owned by Jack McKeddie (brother of George McKeddie, Scottish patriarch of the McKeddie / Cubillo family.) and boss diver Ponsie Cubillo who was Jack McKeddie's nephew. The McKeddie / Cubillos owned shops in Mitchell Street where Shenanigan's is now located.

Valentine said that Mr McKeddie bought the car for his son Jack. The question could be asked how this could have happened with the policy that restricted the rights of Aboriginal people regarding personal ownership of property. One theory was that the names McKeddie and Cubillo eluded the notice of the authorities but that's now history. Jack McKeddie was the son of Annie *Djuan*, a Larrakia woman and George McKeddie a man of financial standing, who owned a huge boarding house on the corner of Mitchell and Peel Streets. Ponsie was the son of Lilly McKeddie, Jack McKeddie's sister married Antonio Cubillo.

Jack McKeddie married Victoria Dashwood who was the sister of George (*Moongooloo*). George also known as George Edwards because he worked for Roy Edwards.[22] George *Moongooloo* Edwards was always immaculately dressed in whites, in his role of working for Roy Edwards family. George *Moongooloo*, his wife *Argeebah*, and his sisters Victoria and Rosie were tribally connected to *Ulyndubu or Ulñyunduboo* Lucy McGinness. Victoria Dashwood was Jack McGinness' tribal aunty while Jack McKeddie was Poncie Cubillo's uncle so culturally speaking their relationship could be considered more family than friend.

Quite apart from their tribal affiliation, music was the common thread that bound the Cubillo and McGinness families together. They were notable musicians in their own respective right.

Music: The International Communicator

Music held a special place in the McGinness family. The most outstanding musician of the McGinness family was Valentine Bynoe who played the steel guitar, mandolin and button accordion. Valentine played for dances in pre-war Darwin and post war for dances and social events in Queensland.

There is a family story that tells how Valentine learnt to play the mandolin. It states that Jack was given a mandolin by his friend Ponsie Cubillo with the hope he would be able to play in time. Jack loved music but was not musical in that sense but was willing to try. Val would steal moments with the mandolin when Jack was away and became very talented with the instrument. The Darwin Mills

---

22   Roy Edwards is no relation to Harry Edwards.

Sisters, Jack's grand children, with their parents have nurtured the music as a tribute to Valentine.

Barney's children also were known to sing and play musical instruments. Micky, Barney's son, was the most notable playing the gum leaf using a folded cigarette packet. Margaret's daughter Ida has a Diploma in music playing the violin and on occasional trips to her beloved Darwin she has played with the Darwin Symphony Orchestra.

Darwin String Band, c1930. Musicians include members of the Cubillo, Damaso, Ah Matt and Lopez families. (Unknown, NTAS, Charles Wilson Collection, NTRS 3335 Item 330).

Having clarified the relationships between the McGinness and the Cubillo families we can return to Jack McKeddie's car. This story as told by Valentine McGinness relates to a journey by some young men in the car. The young men were approached to assist a visiting priest, Brother Francis, who was searching for someone in the Northern Territory. As Catholics and willing to help the priest, Valentine McGinness, and the Cubillo and Damaso boys went with them, journeying down towards Roper River. Val, being a backyard mechanic, was handy to have on board. They got as far as Strangeways Well on the way to Roper Valley where they broke down. They left the priest with the car and went on foot to get help. While they were gone it is said the priest got thirsty and out of desperation he drank some embrocation solution that he had with him in the car. He almost died. That was a bad experience for them which the young men never forgot. They joked about it in later years because the radiator was full of water.

Eventually they didn't feel too bad because they were told that the man was not a priest searching for one of his flock at all but rather a man from Scotland Yard working undercover who was looking for a fugitive.

The little band of Ponsie, Lawrence Cubillo, Babe Damaso, Val McGinness and *Taboogboong* (a *Dutjurrutj* man, coastal neighbours to *Koongurrukuñ*.) all broke up in Katherine where Jack McKeddie's car broke down. Ponsie left for Sydney and Jack never saw him again but caught up with his wife Christina when he went down south some years later.

Many years later and by pure accident I had the pleasure of meeting one of Ponsie's daughters at the State Funeral of Charles Perkins but that's another story in itself.

The Trade Union Movement

In 1923, when Jack was 21, he joined the trades and labor movement that was developing at the time. It remains a mystery how he was able to join, because neither the rules of the Northern Territory Workers Union nor the North Australian Industrial Union [more likely Jack joined NAIU] did not allow for Aboriginals to be members. In 1927 these unions merged to become the North Australia Workers Union (NAWU). He remained a financial and participating member up until his retirement in 1968. Superannuation should have provided him with a nest egg on his retirement but he refused to join based on his earlier experience with the trust account, believing that he would not receive anything and that the Government would benefit.

During the mid 1920s Jack made a visit to Melbourne where Harry Edwards and Margaret his sister were living. On his return to Darwin Jack took up the challenge of fighting injustice once more. He began to pick up where he left off with the effects of the unrest caused by a delegation from Kahlin which had helped keep the main issues on the board. Life for Jack was once again emerging as a freedom seeker, mover and shaker and strong advocate for the underdog and disadvantaged. He was a conscientious objector to the unfair rules that determined people's lives whether they were driven by Government or Public Authority. This was also a period when Jack's personal life changed.

Love in the Air

Then the time came when love was in the air for Jack when a couple of ladies, whose names will not be revealed, were in his sights but racial overtones and political boundaries were in place preventing cross-cultural marriages. He never passed first base with these young ladies which was home visits and going to the movies and sporting events where he could demonstrate his sporting prowess. Purely for

Jungung

the interest of the reader the ethnic backgrounds of these potential girlfriends were diverse: Anglo Saxon, Greek, Spanish Portuguese and Filipino. To add insult to injury, permission to marry was subject to approval by the Chief Protector who had ultimate power over the lives of Aborigines according to *The Act*.

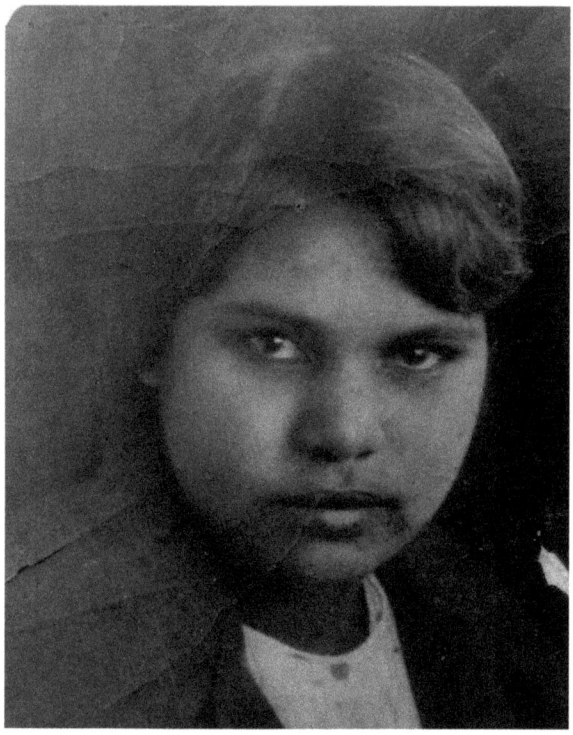

Violet 'Polly' Wakelin, aged 19. (Unknown, Mills Collection).

One can only assume that Jack was not too serious about any of the women concerned or that would have been the battle of the century. Not to say that when he did find the girl he wanted that it was a piece of cake. It was after Jack's return trip from Melbourne that he met the love of his life, Violet Wakelin, and he set about making approaches to the Authorities to marry her.

Violet was also removed from her homelands surrounding Wave Hill Station where she was picked up and sent to Kahlin Compound. Violet's background was of *Guringi/Mudburru* and she claimed that her place of birth was the Kimberley region. As a ward of the state and subject to the total control the *Native Affairs Act*. Violet's fate was to be married off to any potential non-Aboriginal male who offered to marry a Kahlin girl. In return the girls were assured accommodation and government employment. Some of the marriages were lasting while others ended with disastrous results. Much similar to Jack's story, Violet had been taken by her charges to Melbourne and was working in a Local Government residence on her return. She was employed at the time as a house girl and companion nanny and the story Jack tells is that Violet's charges were more stubborn to deal with than the Authorities.

Violet could not have left the compound of her own free will. She was bound by *The Act* and her only hope to leave there would be if she were to get married. Most of her time of incarceration was spent with Government families as house maid and nanny. Violet also travelled south with her sponsor family and on her return she worked for a family who occupied the house below Fort Hill before meeting Jack.

Young Half-caste women could not live independently outside the compound without visible means of support or under a sponsorship family. Those who did survive were recorded as incorrigibles and living in suspicious circumstance. The only way out was if Violet were to marry a European. This was arranged and consented to by the Superintendent of the compound and signed by the Chief Protector of Aborigines. Consent did not mean that people could make their own choice and approval was subject to strict conditions. Marriages between Aboriginals were not encouraged as it conflicted with Dr Cecil Cook's, Chief Protector of Aborigines and Chief Medical Officer, policy of genetic engineering (breeding the colour out).[23]

Jack set his sights on Violet Wakelin and consequently found himself entangled in yet more government red tape. In order to meet the conditions of Dr Cook's policy he had to prove to the authorities his ability to provide for Violet by being in full time employment with a place to live before permission was granted for Violet to leave the control of the Authorities. An impossible task it seemed, knowing that the odds were stacked against him.

However, he was able to do just that, only to face another issue that had the ability to prevent them being married. This was the fact that Jack was Catholic and Violet was Protestant. The rules of the Catholic Church required Violet to be confirmed a Catholic but she refused. Subsequent to this, marriages were not accepted between Catholic and Protestant couples and were outlawed and all efforts were used to discourage it.

This became a minor problem and as I recall it being said, they decided to get married in the Registry Office in 1927.[24] However it did not release them from the obligations of *The Act*.

---

23 Stephen, *Contact Zones*, 197-198.
24 The NT Office of Birth Deaths & Marriages, confirmed that Jack and Violet married on 2 July 1927. Unknown., NT Births, Deaths & Marriage, Personal communication, telephone conversation, 30 April 2019.

They still remained wards of the state and subjects under *The Act* which meant that their freedom could be revoked at any time for whatever reason. To be able to carry out his obligation Jack had to have a permanent job so he joined the North Australian Railways and headed for Katherine and points south to begin his life as a married man.

Sport & Australian Rules Football

Throughout the 1920s sport was an important part of Jack's life as it offered him as well as other Aboriginal men the opportunity to socialise, be engaged in competition and demonstrate sportsmanship and practical skills. The game of Australian Rules was developing with great interest as a Top End sport and the so called 'Coloured men' took to football 'like ducks to water.' Reuben Cooper, one of the 'Coloured men' at that time, had been sent down south by his dad who was a buffalo shooter and introduced the other Aboriginal men to football when he returned. Vesteys Meatworks sponsored a team and both Jack and Reuben played for Vesteys. Other team members included his mate Ponce and Eddie Cubillo, Harry Hazlebane and Putt Ah Matt. Family history records that Jack captained the team in 1920/21, winning the club's first premiership. It was celebrated as a victory for the locals, 'all good sports are pleased to see a young team (mostly composed of boys born and bred in the Territory) come into their own at last. They have always played a fast clean game.'[25] Jack also won the Northern Territory Football League most improved award for the 1923/24 season.

Football provided the opportunity to be competitive and at the same time it served as a launching pad into society. Being based in Katherine, Jack and Timmy Angeles played for the local Katherine team. When Jack was needed he would travel up to Darwin arriving just before the game started.

Games were played at the Esplanade Oval. Mr Bob Murray, the train engineer would toot the whistle a certain way to let people know Jack was on board so his name could be put on the team sheet. The first whistle was at Salonika crossing, after leaving the Two and a half mile siding at Parap, then again as it approached the cutting at the Daly Street bridge. The final toot was on the approach of the Railway Station at Hornibrooks, keeping in step with regulations. Bob Murray, was a staunch unionist and one of Jack's great supporters.

---

25   *NTTG*, 21 February 1922.

A New Life in Darwin During the 1920s

Vesteys Football Club Premiers 1921-22. Back row L-R: George Wedd, Jack McGinness, Bill Nuttall, Roy Green, Bob Anthony, George Tindall, Kevin Dempsey Middle row L-R: Horace Nelson, "Fatty" Harris, Reuben Cooper (Capt.), Harry Hazelbane, Alec Barnett Front row L-R: "Tassie" Graham, William "Putt" Ah Matt, Duncan Presley, Ponce Cubillo. (Unknown, NTG Photographer Collection, NTL, PH0136/0096)

Other men working on the railway playing for Vesty's were George Tindle, Tassie Graham and Bob Anthony. The rest of the team members were also close friends and included; Duncan Presley, Harold Nelson, Fatty Harris and even the little umpire Alan McGuire were friends with them. Jack joked about the boys dunking Alan at Mindil beach next day if they happened to be beaten on the day. This offered the men the opportunity to stand as equals on the field of sport. However, Darwin was not ready for Aboriginal participation in competition sport and therefore they were not openly encouraged. Resistance by racial slurring was part of the scene and sledging in the form of a ditty was a catch cry.

> The blue and whites the dirty sights
> They can't come out of a Saturday night

This was in reference to the so called coloured boys being subject to a curfew and living in Kahlin Compound and other controlled environments. Their reply to that was a political statement of equality,

Jungung

> Who are, who are, who are we
> We are the boys of the VFC (Vesteys Football Club)
> We don't drink coffee and we don't drink tea
> We Drink Beer

This stanza has carried through as one of the chants to their successive present day team Darwin Football Club with the variation

> *Who are, who are, who are we*
> We are we are the Buffaloes
> B - u - double f - a - l - o - e - s
> Buffaloes

Today many of the footballers playing for the Darwin Football Club and other clubs in Darwin are third and fourth generation descendants of the members of the Vesteys Team.

Vesteys Football Club, Most Improved medal. Presented to Jack McGinness for the 1923/24 season. (Medals in keeping of the Ludwig family, Mills Collection.)

A New Life in Darwin During the 1920s

Verses from "History of the Darwin Football Club" by K Mills 1982.[26]

    18, Because this team of yesterday were champions one and all
　　　The names back then live on today as proudly we recall
　　　Names like

    19, Cooper, Tindal, Hazelbane
　　　McGinness, Green, AhMatt
　　　Presley, Edwards, Nuttall, Nelson
　　　Cubillo, Anthony, and Lew Fatt

    20, Pons, Bonson, May and Villaflor
　　　Tye, Graham, Wright and Moo
　　　Damaso, Tybell, Talbot, Motlop
　　　McLennon, Roman, Snape, and Muir

    39, There's future heros still to come
　　　The young ones here today
　　　Will add more names to keep Buffs strong
　　　To them we leave our song

    40, The song about some mighty teams
　　　This song we'll teach to you
　　　It's full of grand tradition
　　　Of the mighty Double Blues

    41, We sing "Old Buffaloes never die"
　　　They only fade away
　　　Then the legend of their names return
　　　When their sons come out to play

It was found that breaking down the social barriers was also needed in competition sport. Jack and his team mates created their own special approach to socializing through sports. Yet another hurdle for them to overcome became a less than perfect opportunity where they could play by the rules and plan a strategy to be recognized as equals. They certainly proved to be more than equal on the footy field but then had to contend with the Colour Bar that existed then which denied them the opportunity to fully integrate.

26　These are verses [numbered] from a longer poem, 'History of the Darwin Football Club' by K Mills.

Katherine high-level railway bridge under construction, c1925. (Unknown, NTL, Paul France Collection, PH0140-0020.)

Katherine Rail Construction Team, c1926. Standing L-R: J Webb, L Rogers, Jack McGinness **[Captain on the day of the 'walk-off']**, Bob Lee, Jim Cox, Harry Brooks, Stew Coates; Front L-R: J Doherty, Norman O'Neil, C Cressy, Ted Rogers, Tim Angeles, J Rogers, J Gibson, Joseph Callahan (team mascot, running across front of photo). (Unknown, Hilary Rowe Collection, NTAS, NTRS 234/ CP348/5)

Katherine railway bridge completed. This is the first train to cross Katherine Railway bridge in January 1926. There was no ceremony to mark the completion, this is simply a work train. (Fletcher, V., NTL, Harold Snell Collection, PH0233-0020).

In December 1926 Jack was the captain of the Katherine Football team when he ordered his team to walk off the field due to unfair decisions brought against them.[27] As a result the Vestey's Football Club, from which the Katherine team drew many of its players, and its coloured players were barred from playing in the competition but not so the white men in the Vesteys team. Jack claimed that Vesteys did not support them so Jack and their supporters formed a new football league known as the Darwin Football League. Darwin football was split along racial lines in what became known as the 'Colour Bar.' The Northern Australia Football League with its constitution banning players of non European descent competed with the multi racial Darwin Football League for three consecutive Darwin football seasons from 1927/28 to 1929/30. This is a remarkable period in Australian Football History and was an early example of the value of sports in the fight for human rights.

When the Colour Bar finally came to an end the coloured football players rejoined the Northern Territory Football League playing for either the Buffaloes Football Club or the Wanderers Football Club. Jack joined the Buffaloes while Val and Joe played for Wanderers. Due to further racial segregation in the 1930s all the coloured players joined the Buffaloes Football Club and together created the

---

27 *NTTG*, 24 December 1926.

'Buffalo Legends.'[28] Many of the descendants of the Buffalo Legends of the 1930s play for the Darwin (Buffaloes) Football Club today.

Football offered the ideal passage forward for Jack and other coloured boys and although the authorities did not resist their inclusion and interaction they did little about the resistance that they were experiencing. All the players were striving for was to be treated as equals. So much for the policy that was meant to promote assimilation through integration. As Jack pointed out, the authorities failed to recognise that the Aboriginal men were actually promoting the principle of assimilation through their efforts to be included.

Disparaging as it may have been at times their humour showed through in the nicknames they gave each other, some of which are worth mentioning;

- Jack McGinness was Broody, being said that he was like a broody hen that once he got hold of the ball you couldn't get the damn thing off him.
- Val McGinness, Hookie, was said to be able to pull a ball in from what seemed to be impossible angles
- Joe McGinness was Turtle, known for his measured play and Sweet Joe because he was a goal sneak which pleased the supporters.
- Putt Ah Matt was Mae West due to his small compact figure and huge chest muscles
- Walter Lew Fatt was Sock because of the certain way he rolled down his socks
- Bill McLennen was Spud. The men all teased each other regarding their characteristics and Spud stuck to Bill.
- Ainkin Ah Matt had several names: Syke, Teat and Tilcos.
- Bali Angeles was Aswang.
- Andy Snape was YardumYardum

Andy's nickname came about following a police raid on a gambling school held at the back of a hotel to which the Aboriginal men would defy the authorities to sneak out to.

When the Constabulary did their rounds the gamblers would all scurry off into the darkness to escape. Unbeknown to the players, the hotel decided to build a tennis court in the back yard and they only got as far as building the fence. That night the police caught the gamblers because they were fenced in. Andy was one of those people hence the word "YardumYardum" meaning they were yarded up. There are many more tales but they will have to be told another time.

---

28 For a full history of the 'Colour Bar' and its aftermath See Stephen, *Colour Bar.*

Buffaloes, c1930. Standing L-R: Victor Brown (in white singlet), Jaffa Ah Matt, Andy Snape, **Jack McGinness**, Don McMillan, Ron Pryor, Marsie Ah Matt, John Ah Matt, Charles Snape. Squatting middle row L-R: Harold Nuttall, Walter Lew Fatt, Arthur Wright, Richard 'Dick' Butler, Don Bonson, Tim Angeles. Sitting L-R: Val Litchfield, William 'Putt' Ah Matt, Lopez 'Johnny' De La Cruz, Basil 'Babe' Damaso, Jacky Lee, Joe Sevallos. (Unknown, Charles Wilson Collection, NTAS, NTRS 3335 Item 342).

Wanderers, c1930. **Joe McGinness** is second from the left in the front row. Other Darwin families represented include Hazelbanes, Cubillos, Jans and McLennan. (Unknown, Charles Wilson Collection, NTAS, NTRS 3335 Item 341).

Jungung

Darwin Buffaloes Football Club League team official photo, 2018/19. Back row L-R: Shaun Pearce President, Kelvin Williams, Edward Trupp, David Johnston, Chris Atkinson, David Paull, Adam Sambono, Kevin Moroney, Richard Russell Asst Coach, Chris Williams, Greg Bain Asst Coach, Tom Fleay. Middle row L-R: Neil Gibson Runner, Tony Williams Committee, Victor Williams, Patrick Boles, Malcolm Rosas, Joe Anderson, Jalen Clarke, Marty Corrie, Brayden Culhane, Daryl White, Chelsea Mulcahy Trainer, Jenna Vermeulen Trainer, Tim Bycroft Water, Costa Karaolias Secretary. Front row L-R: James Verdon, Bill Feeney Asst Coach, Zak Stephenson, Paul Campbell, Cameron Stokes, Matt Campbell Coach, Jarrod Stokes, Shaun Ah Matt, Jackson Clark, Bradley Mitchell, Bradley Stokes, Tim Eldridge, Karen Cardona Social Media.
(Unknown, Courtesy of the Darwin Football Club).

Chapter 5

Katherine: The House That Jack Built

House and yard plan sketch by Simon Scally, date unknown.
(Simon Scally, Mills Collection).

Jack joined the railway after his marriage and so his life with Violet followed the work. Their living quarters were in tents and makeshift accommodation along the railway line near to where he was employed. Their movements can be traced by the birth of the children. The eldest daughter Joyce was born at the King River siding, Violet in Mataranka, Sadie in Darwin, Mildred (Mim) in Birdum, Kathleen, Joan and Marie in Katherine. The two boys were born after the war broke out. Brian was born in Balaklava in South Australia during the war and Raymond was born after the family's return to Katherine.

During the construction work on building and maintenance of the line between Birdum and Katherine, living in tents proved to be too hard for Jack and his small family. He decided that he would buy a block of land in First Street in Katherine to ensure a more stable life for his family and Katherine in 1930, or thereabouts, became their permanent home. It was the place where his strength of character really developed and his reputation as a leader grew as a person of note. He was a hard worker and earned the respect of all who knew him taking on the establishment for the protection of his family and others. Life for his family was as comfortable as was possible for Jack. He worked very hard to make that happen in order to care and keep them away from the authorities.

The house was a fairly substantial home for that period as building materials were scarce and hard to come by. The house had a major living area with two bedrooms on either side, front and back closed in verandahs, and a small kitchen, which was an extension off the back verandah. The material used was largely Ironwood and Cyprus pine pillars as framework support and timber struts for wall panels and window frames. Corrugated iron was used for the exterior walls with bamboo slats for verandah panels and push-out windows.

On the approach to the front door was a large trellis covered with bougainvillea and what we called "Chinese lantern". The back verandah consisted of an elongated trellis which provided the house with protection from the afternoon sun. The verandahs provided a breeze-way with a gabled ceiling as a form of ventilation and cooling system.

The main living and visitor area was the front verandah, with a sealed polished cement floor and where the Beale piano was situated. The middle section contained a large dining table that took pride of place with a fine Damask tablecloth for special occasions. Opposite the dining table sat a cabinet radio powered by a car battery and the much adored His Masters Voice Gramophone on a separate cabinet. The battery operated wireless with its small insulator aerial passed through the wall and extended to a high branch of a gum tree close by.

The kitchen floor was cemented and the major bedroom was half cement and wood floor. The girls' bedroom was not cemented because work was interrupted by the outbreak of World War II. Had this not occurred, Jack's idea of making a floor out of crushed ant bed and polished by glazing would have eventuated. Antbed floors were being widely used and people were experimenting with all sorts of ideas for building at that time. Jack was an innovator and was always happy to try new things.

There were two large trees in the back yard with a swing hanging from a beam strung between the branches. One of the trees was a white gum and the other was what we called the butterfly tree because the seeds with splayed edges looked like butterflies. Jack placed pieces of old tyres in the forks where the beams rested to protect the trees from the rubbing action caused by the swing.

Katherine: The House That Jack Built

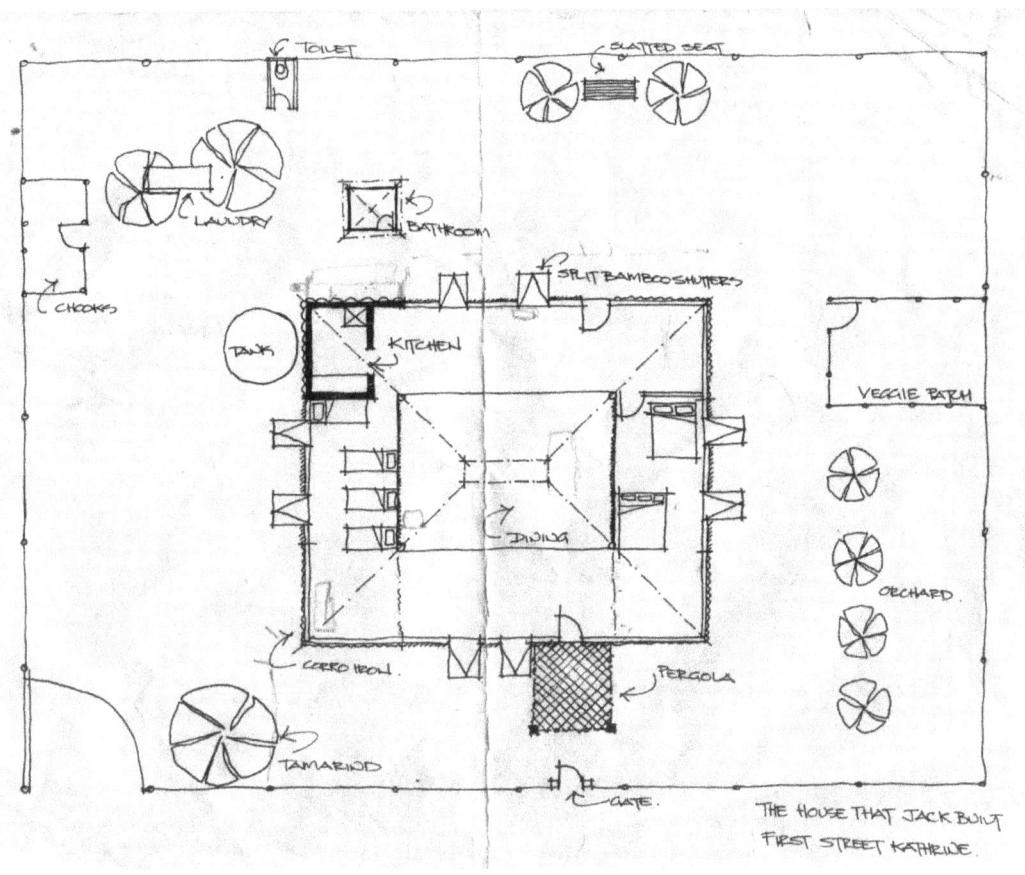

House plan, date unknown. (Simon Scally, Mills Collection).

I [Kathy] remember we had corn, we had pumpkins, we had custard apple, we had pineapples, we had Chinese cabbage, we had everything. And here's this man, actually building us this house. We had water, you know, the taps and showers, and everything—we had our own shower. And I just marvel at him being able to do that as well as any non-Aboriginal person in Katherine. I would say that we had one of the most substantial houses in the Katherine area

Because of restrictions in the Act, Aboriginal relations were forbidden by law from entering our house. When I reflect and look back, I think how terrible it was that our Grandmother and our family couldn't come into our house. But we didn't know that at the time. But I think how horrible it must've been for Mum and Dad too, who knew how much that grated on them, that they couldn't have the people in their house. They wouldn't have prevented them from going into the house at any time, but the old people respected that and they wouldn't stay.

Jungung

> *Even when we went through our ceremonies, our cultural ceremonies, they wouldn't mark us. When I say mark, that's something that you can see scars on people, those initiation scars and that.[29] They wouldn't, what they called mark us, so that it would be visible to the authorities. We went through the same principle and the same initiation ceremony, but not actually cutting your skin, and doing that thing to raise a mark.*
>
> *So, our old people understood that ¾ they didn't want to get Mum and Dad into trouble, they didn't want to get us children into trouble, but they still wanted to carry out their responsibilities with us.*
>
> *And it's very sad now, when I think about it, how we were forced to treat our people like that, but as I said, it wasn't something that we enjoyed doing and it must've been terrible for my Mum and Dad.[30]*

There was a sanitary cart that operated at the time but Jack serviced his own needs by building a pit toilet in the far corner of the yard. These outdoor toilets were known as flaming furies because they were routine doused in kerosene and set alight. The shower and laundry were separate from the house under a huge white gum tree. The fowl house skirted one side of the fence and the vegetable patch was situated along the fence line on the opposite side. Most people who owned their homes had a fowl house as an essential requirement not solely for eggs as a food supplement but also to use the manure as fertiliser for the garden.

In much later years Jack would be called on to recite the following poem and then the other rendition which became very much in demand at parties and other functions.

The house that Jack built at 21 First Street, Katherine, c 1930.
(Unknown, Mills Collection).

---

29 The 'markings' are cicatrisation or *Budaru* in *Koongurrukuñ*.
30 Mills, Kathy, Personal communication with Matthew Stephen, 24 May 2019. Kathy could not recall where this quote was originally documented.

No.1 Version;

This is the house that Jack built

This is the malt that lay in the house that Jack Built

This is the rat that ate the malt that lay in the house that Jack built

This is the cat that killed the rat that ate the malt that lay in the house that Jack built etc etc

No.2 Version;

This is the domicile that was erected by John

This is the fermented grain that lay in the domicile that was erected by John

This is the member of the rodent species that masticated the fermented grain that lay in the domicile that was erected by John

This is the member of the feline species that annihilated the member of the rodent species that masticated the fermented grain that lay in the domicile that was erected by John etc etc etc

Young Jack McGinness. (Unknown, Mills Collection).

Taking Polly home

Once settled in Katherine, Jack decided to take Violet, or Polly as she was also known to family and friends, back home to see her mother and family who were then living on Wave Hill Station. This was the first opportunity Violet had to return to her homeland after she had been taken away. Jack had an old Ford Tin Lizzy and that is how he took his family to meet his in-laws. It is remarkable to think of the effort needed to do the trip with three young children; Joyce, Violet and Sadie, with mother Violet expecting her fourth child Mildred. There were no petrol stations between Katherine and Wave Hill and they followed the old stock and station route that went through Cow Eye Crossing, a branch of the King River. Violet found her mother and reunited with other members of her family and people and her country of birth.

Tin Lizzie in the NT outback, c 1920s. (Unknown, Victoria Musuem, The Biggest Family Album in Australia, MM 6772).

Ulñyunduboo, Lucy McGinness lived in Katherine with the family from time to time and would have assisted with the births of the girls, along with other Aboriginal grannies who may have been present at these important times. When Lucy was not with Jack she lived with Barney and his family in Darwin.

Standing L-R: Violet 'Polly' McGinness & Margaret Edwards.
In front L-R: Joyce McGinness and Ida Edwards (Later Bishop),
Katherine, c 1930s. (Unknown, Mills Collection).

Home births were usual for most people during this era and it never surprised Jack to come home and be presented with an addition to the family. In later days he would wonder at the classified ads in the newspaper announcing the birth of a child and the comment "Mother and baby doing well". He had never been aware of any problems and therefore saw no reason why things should not turn out well. But there must have been occasions when things did not work out ideally, which men were more or less oblivious to. Full credit must be given to the women who worked beside their menfolk and endured the same hardship and disadvantages for the sake of their marriage and children. Historically, husbands were spared the added worry of any discomfort experienced by their women and Jack was no exception.

The differing Catholic and Protestant religious practices caused some concerns for Jack and Violet but not a lot. Baptism and confirmation was a shared agreement so those children who happened to be born during the time a visiting Catholic priest came through Katherine were baptized a Catholic. Any other children were christened by the regional Aboriginal Inland Mission priest who happened to be a Methodist. This arrangement seemed to work and never caused any major problems as both Jack and Violet saw some resemblance between the spirituality in European religion and Aboriginal spirituality which both were denied the right to practice. Mildred, Joan and I were baptized Catholics by the visiting priest. Fathers Gsell, McGraff and Henschke were well known to the Territory at this time. The legendry Tim O'Shea, owner of the Katherine Hotel, and his family were devout Catholics and as part of their obligation to the Catholic Church supported and participated as sponsors in the Baptism ceremonies. My sponsor God Mother was his daughter Shelagh and I was named Kathleen after another of his daughters. The McGinness family was known as a Catholic family even though some of us, heaven forbid, were in fact Protestant!

It should be understood that at that particular time there were strict rules against marriages and social interaction between Catholics and Protestants. The first generation McGinness children in the Old Country represented the Orange and the Green from their own beginning and this flowed on into the next generation through the Native Affairs and the Caste system. The whole family went without prejudice to Sunday school with Mr Long of the Aboriginal Inland Mission because both Jack and Violet believed in the moral principles of Christianity. Whenever a Catholic priest came to Katherine the Catholics in the family attended the mass with Jack as part of his duties to his own church and religious obligations to his children. Jack never resisted the split loyalties. However, when he felt peeved he claimed that the Methodists were bigger wowsers than the Catholics

Bent Nails, Pieces of String and Bits of Wire

Jack had a family of seven girls to contend with, but the girls were included in all the activities in and around the dwelling. There was a tree planted in the yard for each child which made up a grove of Poinciana down the side of the house to provide shade to the bedroom and Horseradish trees were planted around the front yard to shade the recreation areas. Each child had to care for their own tree by keeping it watered and help mother with the flowering shrubs of oleander or fairy trees as we called them. Butterflies wove cocoons on the underside of the leaves. The cocoons had beautiful colours which the children believed were fairy lanterns. Flowerbeds of Zinnia and Billy Goat Stinkers skirted the front fence and the Mountain Rose Magnificent draped over the side fence. The vegetable garden was Jack's, while the fowl house was the domain of Polly and the older girls. There was a natural plant section as well as an attempted recreation of the plants gathered from the billabong. Mildred had a hospital for wounded grasshoppers and *pubootj* (bush potato) patch.

The girls became Jack's off-siders when he needed help and became very apt in knowing which tool he would need for particular jobs such as soldering etc. They were much like surgical nurses ready with the right instrument depending on the job.

Jack could never pass up a piece of timber that he thought would come in handy later. He had a special tin for bent nails, bits of wire and pieces of string that were considered prized finds in the days when hardware stores did not exist. There was no adhesive tape for wrapping parcels so everything had to be tied with string. Collecting those items became a habit that was taken up by his children. In less busy times Jack and his helpers would gather as a group using the bootlast to straighten the nails. Bruised thumbs and blood blisters on little dainty fingers were quite common in "The House That Jack Built".

Ponds cream was a great magic potion for bruised fingers. This was carefully administered by Polly. When mixed with talcum powder it was used as a soothing skin balm, purely for cosmetic and for comfort. All those fingers were needed to do much more delicate needle work, the ever-present necessity for domestic training, social etiquette and preparing personal Glory Boxes. All the girls were fine needle-workers and the craft continues on in Mim, whose embroidery and knitting was often seen in craft displays at the Royal Darwin Show. Joyce was great at embroidery and fine crotchet work especially making the edges for personal handkerchiefs. She learnt to knit during the war period. She became very adept at knitting, especially her fair-isle and cable stitches, which were considered to be very difficult to master.

Domestic Responsibility & Plaiting the Grass

On many hunting trips when the tall spear grass seemed impenetrable Jack took the lead and plaited the grass with his feet to make a pathway which all could follow. The grass was not trampled and the followers single file walked on the mat of folded grass and not the bent edges so that the grass would be able to correct itself after a period of time.

On the return journey after a long day the exit clearly showed the route to be taken with the flattened grass beginning to straighten itself. This was part of the bush survival skills Jack had learned while being taught in bush law in the way of the land during his youth on his native land at *Mudgidirbirr* Bynoe Harbour area. When applied to life, basic bush survival skills are invaluable for those who wish to journey towards their own destiny. If the destination is not what is expected then there is the opportunity to return fully understanding the way one arrived. Physically plaiting the grass as passed on by Jack as an important bush survival skill is now symbolic philosophy for his family in knowing the way, arriving at the desired destination and knowing how to return. In later years and in questionable situations his family adopted the phrase 'We might have to plait the grass, people.'

Jack was elected to the town council before the outbreak of World War II and was heavily involved in the Katherine community. He was not the favourite 'John Citizen' when he and a young friend Jackie Freeman, wrote a letter to the council protesting against the local Police Sergeant keeping his herd of goats in the town area by placing an ad in the *NT Gazette*. Polly was equally respected for community work caring for the pensioners around the town and visiting the compound and always taking parcels of material, needles and thread. Some of the elderly people had ingrown eyelashes and Polly would tend to them and remove the lash if necessary. Despite some resistance from a certain quarter of the community Violet became a member of the Country Women's Association.[31] They adopted Katherine as their home and both contributed to the community wherever needed.

Jack and 'Polly' with Joyce, Violet, Sadie at house 21 First St, Katherine, c1930s. (Unknown, Mills Collection).

---

31   Ogden, *Women of Katherine*, 161.

Their children were no less involved and included in social events around town. These activities included delivering meals made by Polly for the old pensioners such as Bill Roberts and Bill McGregor, who lived alongside the railway bridge near to where Charlie Beer and his family lived.

There is an area on the banks of the Katherine River known as McGregor's hole just below where Mr McGregor had his house.

The old pensioners in turn would send parcels of vegetables they had grown, custard apple and bananas which were always a welcome treat. Trombone pumpkin was a specialty along with broad bean and New Guinea bean which were grown over bowers as an outdoor shade area. We often wondered why our mother did that and were told that the men had no families to help care for them. We didn't have our grandfathers so we understood their situation was comparable to ours. I first heard mention of Remittance Men when I was quite young and perhaps one or two men living in Katherine fitted that description. It wasn't until later years that I got to appreciate what the term meant. They were men who were sent out to various colonies for purposes known only to their family who were responsible for the arrangement. In effect they were financed exiles from their family.

Other identities living in Katherine were Jim Douglas, Jack Campbell, Fred Prior, Harry Cousins, an Italian named Peter Violi, and Alf Winkup who was a Norwegian. There was a real mixture of people, Russian, German, Chinese and Aboriginal which added to the multi-national population of Katherine. The McGinness children grew up in such an environment and became quite versatile in understanding the different accents of speakers. At one end of the street I was called Katarina Marianna and the other end it was Kathleen Mavournan. "Aye than, hav yuh bin a good lass fer yur mither, now, hav yuh?" asked Tim O'Shea. "Aye, that I have," was the expected response but "yes Pop" was accepted which sometimes was rewarded with a Mintie.[32]

Jack took turns in cutting down a Christmas tree for the Town Hall and we went with him when he would head south down the Track towards Mataranka to find a suitable tree for the Christmas party. The way he would choose the tree, which was usually a Cypress Pine, is still talked about within his family. He was such a bugger for detail, as was crudely expressed choosing a Christmas tree was no exception.

Approaching Christmas each year Jack would load up the old Tin Lizzy with a saw, adze and an axe and head off down The Track towards Mataranka, a small

---

32 Minties are a mint flavoured confectionary.

township 107 kilometres south of Katherine.[33] On the way there were natural outcrops of Lancewood and Cyprus pine on either side of The Track which made the journey a pleasant one. One would imagine that the first tree sighted would be the one he chose, not so. He would park the car in a shady spot and get the children to help set up an area for a little picnic. While they rested he would survey the groves of trees until he found one suitable for the all important event of Christmas in the Town Hall. It had to be the right size and shape according to Jack's thumb rule and there was nothing else to consider except the decorations, which he left to the experts in that department. After settling on the right tree he would fell the tree, saw off the branches that he didn't think were needed and then hone the rough edges with the adze. The tree was then loaded onto the tray back of the old Tin Lizzie and taken back to Katherine where it would be decorated by the ladies committee.

Everyone in and around Katherine would come to town for Christmas and the children would receive their presents and refreshments in good community spirit. Many of the presents were home-made toys made by the men and pretty party dresses and pinafores with lace for the girls if available. Women baked for the occasion and the men helped decorate while one would be Father Christmas.

The McGinness house in First Street was a popular stop over for the freight and supply trucks that ran along The Track between Alice Springs and Darwin. The trucks were called DID (Department of the Interior) and commonly known as road trains. Spurgeon Nichols who Jack knew from his footy days in Darwin was in charge of the transport yard in Alice Springs. The drivers were Jack Day and Jack King and they drove the supply trucks to Aboriginal settlements around the Territory. There were no petrol stations apart from a bowser situated outside Rundle's store in the main street. The McGinness house in First Street, Katherine and Mrs Coles' house in Main Street, Tennant Creek, were a welcome relief for the drivers. They offered a rest, a cup of tea, a shower and something to eat.

Other homes, like the two mentioned, broke the long journey and provided an opportunity for travellers to catch up on news and take a much needed rest. In return the drivers, especially Jack King, who was married to Ruby Smith, a cousin to Violet, would take parcels out to Wave Hill Station for her mother and bring news and gifts from them on his return. It was a time when people relied on the convenience of exchange and barter rather than paying by legal tender.

The house was home to many travellers and one in particular was a nineteen year old from NSW who was stranded in Katherine. His name was Jackie Freeman.

---

33 CLA Abbott, Northern Territory Administrator, 1937-1946, first referred to the Stuart Highway during his administration. Up until that time, the main north south road from Darwin was often referred to as 'The Track.'

Jack took him in and gave him a job on the railways with him and the family was pleased because they looked on him as the brother that they never had. Contact was lost during the war until sometime in the sixties his son, also named Jack Freeman, came to Darwin looking for Jack McGinness. Jack junior was 21 at the time and Jack McGinness was back working for the railways at 22 mile. He was so pleased to have met young Jack as was the family.

Jack Freeman & Jack McGinness in front of 21 First St, Katherine, c1930s. (Unknown, Mills Collection).

Another young man who was taken in to the family was Ken McCarthy, a serviceman who is believed to have joined the Australian Navy on his return south. Other young people who were fostered by Jack and Violet were the Saville boys, George, Jacky and Henry, whose father Henry Saville worked as a drover with the droving plant of Charlie Swan. The boys needed schooling and were sent to Katherine for that purpose. Their sister Amy and her daughters Peggy and Beryl were living with Bill Howlett, who eventually did time in Katherine gaol for a firearm offence that injured Amy. Other boys such as Trickler Morgan and *Chunamah* George Woodroofe also had short periods with the McGinness family being *Mudburra* people and culturally related to Violet.

Jungung

The Holtze family was also an important part of the Katherine community.[34] The Holtze family of Mataranka, was another railway family who have been associated with the McGinness family from the early 1920s during the construction of the Katherine Bridge. The Holtze family are descended from the well known Territory identity, Wallaby Holtze, a pioneer in his own right.[35] Every male member of the Holtze family worked for the railways and the women worked for other businesses around Mataranka and Birdum. Dorothy George (Holtze family) worked as a domestic for the O'Shea family who ran the boarding house as did her mother and sisters. We knew her as Trixi, when she was engaged as house girl and nanny to the Millar Children in Katherine. Mr Millar was the Principal of the school in Katherine before World War Two. Teresa was 13 years of age and should have been a student rather than a worker. However, 13 was the working age for young Aboriginal women at that particular time. George Holtze married Alice *Mundolooloo*, a *Ngulakan* woman; Ronnie married Elsie Kilmartin, a *Gurindji* woman and kin to Violet McGinness. Angus married Nancy *Lun Ngynah* a *Jowyon/Youngman* woman. The Holtze families remain living in the Katherine and Darwin region and their extended family is now part of many Darwin and Alice Springs families. The most famous member of the family and son of Dorothy is Bill Dempsey MBE, renowned West Perth footballer.[36] Dorothy's other son John Patterson also became a prominent footballer in Darwin and later took up an executive management position ATSIC, the peak representative body for Aboriginal people in the Northern Territory. John was one time CEO for *Wurli Wulinjang*, the Aboriginal medical service in Katherine. In 2019 he is CEO for the Aboriginal Medical Services Alliance of the Northern Territory (AMSANT). Steven Koops, the son of Joan *Mundalooloo* Koops, followed in the family football tradition, playing for the Fremantle Dockers, 1996-2003 and the Western Bulldogs, 2004.

It is impossible to mention every one that came into contact with Jack during his time in Katherine but it would be remiss to not mention George Kruger.

---

34 Kathy remembers this of Dorothy George (Holtze family). Dorothy was very much a lady, is another person who recognizes the work Jack did and encouraged me to write his story. When I told her that I was writing a book about my father she said, quote; "It's about time someone wrote a book about Jack".
35 Bisa, *Remember Me Kindly: A History of the Holtze Family in the Northern Territory*.
36 Gorman, *Legends: The AFL Indigenous Team of the Century*, 34-49.

George Kruger.

George Edward Kruger
If you ever went to Katherine
You were sure to meet this man
He was tall and straight and honest
and he was known throughout the land

He was as wiry as the Stringy Bark
as tough as Ironwood
and I challenge anybody
that no finer man has stood

He lived there since the birth of Katherine
He helped her grow in years
With his Bungi Jack McGinness
and the other pioneers

They worked on the construction
of the Katherine Railway Bridge
they worked the rail right through to Birdum
With their wives their kids and them

They set the first foundation stone
For their families to live
in harmony together
with those who weren't their kin

George's principles for living
He was never one to lie
His heritage was black and white
This he never did deny

Selina was his mother's name
She came from Pigeon Hole
He was on Buchanan Station
When he was just a child

Jungung

He saw the great big star above
An independant man
Neerabin Nglarile Emu dreaming
He was free to walk his land

But he wore his father's name with pride
That pride he ne'er forgot
Frank Kruger was his father
To whom he owed a lot

He kept his stance throughout his life
as good as any man
Whether working on a cattle station
Or a railway fettler gang

A man of simple living
No desire for wealth or fame
his wealth was in his living
his gnarled hands his fame

George Edward Kruger
Held the history of Katherine in his hands
A first class Territorian
Jack McGinness's greatest pal

K Mills

George Edward Kruger is believed to be the son of Frank Kruger a pioneer who it is said came from Mt Eba in South Australia. According to our oral history Frank Kruger was the first manager of Rundle Store before it became known as Cox Store. The store was situated on the main street at the southern entrance to Katherine next door to the baker shop run by Bill Carter. The McGinness house was built adjacent to the Cox residence on Second Street. The original site is now absorbed by the Woolworth's shopping precinct. It is said that the young apprentice who worked there was a young Cyril Cox, who eventually bought out the store.

Frank Kruger had several interests in the way of property, one being known as the Donkey Camp, upstream from the town beyond the old Telegraph Station and the store at Knotts Crossing.

The common belief was that the place got its name because of the huge herds of donkeys left after the teamster era that supplied the area around the Maude Creek Junction. Donkey Camp was a favourite camping spot for both the Kruger and McGinness families on their regular fishing trips. It had all the evidence of a transport/repair depot with old wagon wheels and spare metal rims and used tools, which made exciting discoveries for the inquisitive mind. There was a depot and workshop where wagon repairs were carried out and this is the place where some of Frank Kruger's other children were born. Looking southwards from the entrance to the Native Compound in Katherine one could see the close proximity to the place of the Big Rainbow Dreaming the place of great significant to the local Aboriginal people. Donkey Camp offered an appropriate setting for the stories of traditional importance.

Jack would prepare the camp site and the children would gather wood for the fire and grass to put under the tarpaulin for the bedding. The fire was lit and a large log was placed across the middle to make good coals for cooking later. There was no commercial bread to take along and Johnny cakes and pufftaloons [fried scones] were the accompaniments for the evening meal. We were fascinated watching our Dad after a day of fishing or hunting making the bread scones which he cooked on the glowing coals. His pet name for them was buggers on the coals. Before retiring we would have story time. Looking up to the star-studded sky we listened to our parents relating their special memories and how the stars and the atmosphere through dreaming stories connected with the earth and the people. One of the most fascinating stories was the story of the Seven Sisters which Jack was connected to in tribal liturgy, and we experienced the relationship between people and the universe. Orion and the Seven Sisters constellation was pointed out to us as we gazed upwards to the stars. The different levels called *Merrwerr* in *Koongurukan* language were connected although separate in their purpose. The different *Merrwerr*, place of existence being the subterranean, the earth, the atmosphere and the stratosphere and how they inter-relate through law and culture in the dreaming.

Before and after the war both the Kruger and McGinness families made regular visit to the Katherine Native compound to catch up with their relations who were placed there. Polly Wurrumburr, the mother of Frank Kruger's other children, lived there with her tribal family after her children to Frank Kruger had been removed and taken to Kahlin Compound in Darwin. There were other relatives and families such as Grannies Bessie Croft, Alice *Boon Boon*, *Nungalah* Nellie and Windham Davy, *Tirryl,* Kitty and *Mun-ngari* to mention but a few. This was a point of annoyance for Jack as he drew comparison with his earlier experience with the Kahlin Compound and he never stopped worrying the authorities over these matters. They in turn never ceased to hound him with threats of police action and not issuing him with a permit to enter The Compound. Jack ignored their threats as he claimed that he was taking his wife and children to visit their relatives, which could be neither proved or disproved one way or the other.

His dislike for one of the Native Affairs Officers never changed because the officer had fathered part Aboriginal children while incarcerating others. Likewise he never accepted the fact his brother Barney worked for the Native Affairs and it caused a great deal of dissent between them whenever the subject was raised. He did not succumb to any persuasion that might change his attitude and vehemently argued that their personal experience of being separated from their mother was grounds enough for Barney to object and that Barney did have the choice to refuse.

However, apart from the contentious issue that lay between them they were as strong as brothers can be, because they knew that being a family was important to their survival as displaced people. Together they defied the authorities and cared for their black mother. Barney brought his family down to Katherine as often as was possible and their political arguments were put aside for pleasurable purposes of camping, fishing and hunting.

George and his family went with the McGinness family on the fishing trips and he told his own stories about his father and his extended family. George was also an exceptional man in his own right stating that Frank Kruger's nationality being originally from the Boer Republic defined George's identity as he jokingly claimed to be Boer-riginal as opposed to Abor-iginal. Similarly, Jack claimed that his father being a British subject should have meant that his identity should be the same as his father's. Needless to say, neither claim was endorsed by the authorities. George Kruger, cultural businessman, stockman, self-taught mechanic, was to become a genuine lifelong friend of Jack's.

They met as young men in the early nineteen hundreds and remained as close friends until their eventual deaths. Jack and George worked on the railways from roughly 1928 to 1950. They both settled in Katherine and brought their entire family up in Katherine. Jack moved to Darwin after the war but George lived out his adult life in Katherine and to date his family continues to live in Katherine.

It was a struggle from the beginning and they had to vie for virtually everything they had. Between them both they had a family that grew together with a bond that stood the test of time. They became true friends and partners and whatever Jack had George had and vice versa. In what was considered to be a critical time for

Aboriginal people in this country they experienced discrimination, incarceration and domination through forced assimilation policies, but these two young men stood back to back against adversity and they set out to prove they were equal to all tasks put before them and that they considered themselves equal to all.

First of all they had to survive the challenge they set for themselves to live independently, support and maintain their family at the same time deal with the control of the all disempowering legislation of the *Native Affairs Act* that both were subject to. It is hard for anyone to imagine what hardship these two young men and their wives went through. After living in tents they gradually secured property and built their own homes. George could not read or write substantially, but what he lacked in formal and written education he made up in wit, wisdom and the art of orating. Together they built their homes, they both owned cars and they both bought property at a time when Aboriginal people were restricted in owning personal possessions. One can only assume that their determination contributed to the apparent change of attitude of the authorities. The authorities may have chosen to overlook the restrictions and treat them as worthy citizens.

George had originally bought land at King River and it became a weekend retreat for the Mac's, and Jack's place was the town house for the Krugers. Both wives assisted with each other's confinements whenever possible, but when Aunty Lily was asked about these things she would give a little giggle and say that she was a coward at first. Lillian Carter was a very young woman fresh out of Emerald River Mission on Groote Eylandt when she married George in 1935. After spending some time with her cousin Gladys Farmer, she was introduced to George, and they were married in Katherine. Their reception was held at the McGinness home in First Street. Their wedding photos were taken in the front yard of the McGinness home but it seems that Cyclone Tracy may have claimed them.

Jungung

L-R: Uncle George Kruger, Jack Gibbs, Young George Kruger, Ali Ah Matt (Unknown, Barbara Raymond Collection).

Chapter 6

World War II

Prime Minister Robert Menzies declared Australia's entry into World War II on 3 September 1939. In Katherine little changed at first other than a small group of soldiers being posted to the town. The town's population was approximately 187.[37] The town was centred on the main street along the north to south highway and along the Katherine River and consisted of two hotels, three stores, one of them being the original store at the old crossing. There were also a number of Chinese traders selling a variety of food and clothing in the main street. A post office, police station, hospital, aerodrome and a small number of private homes completed the township.[38]

Katherine Terrace, Pioneer Store on right, c1940.
(Unknown, NTL, Jim Clarke Collection, PH0105-0104).

The McGinness family in First Street would not have noticed much change in the early years of the war. Jack remained fully involved in community affairs through his involvement in the North Australia Workers Union, trustee of the Katherine Public Hall and community sports.[39] Violet participated in the Katherine branch

---
37 Ogden, *Women of Katherine*, 58.
38 Ogden, *Katherine's Wartime Years, 1942 to 1947*, 1.
39 See re: NAWU, *Northern Standard (NS)*, 25 July 1939, Public Hall. Ogden, P., *Women of Katherine*, 53. *NS*, 2 April 1940. *NS*, 9 May 1941.

of the CWA and looking after her family and the many other local residents that relied on her generosity.[40]

In December 1941 Japan entered the war and this quickly affected the McGinness family in Katherine.

> We didn't really know what a war was. Any awareness of the war was via the 'wireless', but we did recognise the 'signs' of the military build up. The army seemed to arrive in Katherine over night and it looked like 'mushrooms had grown down our street with all the tents.' The army instructed locals to build L shaped slit trenches in our yards and the drill was that when the siren went to all go down in the trenches. At school we were taught that when the siren went we had to run home. My mother did not like us to go in the slit trench because if we were to die they would just cover us over.[41]

On the 12th of December the Australian War Cabinet announced the evacuation of women and children from Darwin. A preliminary census identified that there were 1066 women and 969 children to be evacuated.[42] News of the fall of Singapore on the 15th of February 1942 heightened fears that the war was fast approaching the Northern Territory. On the same day the last evacuation vessel left Darwin, while the last Darwin evacuees left by air on the 18th of February. There was no attempt to evacuate the civilian population of Katherine. News of the Bombing of Darwin on the 19th of February travelled quickly to the town and military activity in Katherine increased almost immediately.

On the 21st of March a Japanese photographic reconnaissance flight flew undetected over Katherine. The following day a flight of nine Mitsubishi G4M1 type 1 Betty bombers left Koepang, Timor bound for Katherine. They arrived over Katherine at 1230, circled overhead twice and then each plane dropped their load of 10 incendiary bombs and anti-personnel bombs, known as 'Daisy Cutters.' The main target was the Katherine air field which was being upgraded by the US Army's 808th Engineers Battalion at the time. 85 bomb craters were counted after the raid while some other bombs fell at Knotts Crossing near a Post Master General line party, the hospital and the Gallon License store.[43]

---

40 Ogden, *Women of Katherine*, 161.
41 Mills, Kathy, Oral History Interview, NTRS 3163 BWF 25_S2_2.
42 NAA guide, *Evacuation of women and children from Darwin, 1941–42*, http://guides.naa.gov.au/records-about-northern-territory/part1/chapter4/4.2.aspx_accessed 06022019
43 Reed & Croft, *The Fall of the Daisy Cutters*, 12.

World War II

Hangars and buildings at the Katherine Aerodrome, c1930s.
The hangar at the rear was mostly used by Dr Clyde Fenton for his Gypsy Moth aircraft – the Flying Doctor Service. The other buildings were mostly used for accommodation for passengers passing through.
(Unknown, Museum Victoria, The Biggest Family Album in Australia, MM1427).

I remember the planes coming in and we were told we had to go through this exercise but we all ran down to the billabong and the silly thing we found later on was that we were going towards that because they were bombing the aerodrome and they were trying to knock out the aerodrome and the big railway bridge. Well we were nearer the railway bridge from where we lived and we would have been in the line of fire if you think about guns coming down the main street of Katherine from the bridge and they could have taken all those houses with shrapnel and goodness knows what. But they were specifically aiming for the bridge because they thought it was the only source of transportation for Darwin, they were going to disable Darwin by cutting off the bridge because they thought that would cut us off from the southern states and all the supplies and that was in line with the railway and everything. So they were targeting that. So we actually saw the dogfights ... Then all of a sudden wherever we went into down to the billabong you could see all this heavy artillery which we never even saw, we just saw the tents and the army men. But wherever they came from with these Ack Ack guns they came right to where we were because it was in line with the aerodrome. And we had that poor old thing, that missionary man, he got shell shock and he was running around and the police, the soldiers said 'Halt' or you'll be shot. They had to warn you. That man was oblivious shaking like a leaf and the army, someone sang out 'someone get that man' because white, you never wear white because it is more easy to see on the ground and they could see where people were so my Dad ran out and grabbed him and rugby tackled him to the ground and took him in to the cover of the bushes where we were. ... Dad, Mum and all the children were there and we all had to put sticks in our mouths. When we were going through the drill at home we'd put those dolly pegs in our mouths, for concussion, for when the bombs went off or you'd bite your tongue off or your jaws or whatever, so the drill was dolly pegs but we went to the bush, we got sticks [laughter], we all had to bite in to the bark and the thing was horrible but we had to keep the sticks in our mouths. ... It was very exciting to us as children, ... it was all over in a flash.

There was only one recorded death as a result of the Katherine bombing raid. An Aboriginal man, Dodger *Kodjalwal*, was killed when he ran from the hospital in fright.[44] Many Katherine residents who witnessed the bombing believed that had the Japanese decided to bomb the town, instead of the Rocks Area, the whole town would have been destroyed with many more fatalities. It was believed that the railway yard was full of trains, all loaded with ammunition, just waiting for the all-clear to proceed further north.[45]

McGinness family being evacuated, c March, 1942. (Unknown, NTL, Alexander Fleetwood Collection, PH0546/0025).

---

44 Schubert, *World War II attacks outside of Darwin need more recognition*.
45 Ogden, *Katherine's Wartime Years*, 3.

Soon after the bombing of Katherine the civilian population was evacuated. On 27 March 1942 162 evacuees left Katherine by train and two days later on 29 March a second group of 61 were also evacuated. On 28 March 152 evacuees left Pine Creek. Most of the evacuees travelled by train to Larrimah and then by truck to Alice Springs.[46]

The McGinness family joined the evacuations as did the family of Kathy's aunty Caroline McGinness and the Kruger family who were evacuated from Katherine by truck. For the children the journey south was an exciting adventure with all the activity of their small convoy. Jack McGinness remained behind in Katherine while his family took almost nothing with them when they left heading south on the Stuart Highway. The Stuart Highway was still just a dirt road at the time although it was sealed later during the war. The evacuees consisted of six of Jack McGinness's daughters, Joyce, Violet, Sadie, Kathy, Joan and Marie and their mother, Mrs Kruger with her 3 children, and Caroline McGinness with her 6 children. Caroline McGinness was expecting a baby at the time and was picked up by the Flying Doctor after having her baby at Dunmarra. When the group reached Alice Springs they transferred to The Ghan for the journey to Adelaide.

> When the train carrying the two McGinness families pulled in to the Adelaide railway station, a porter pulled open the door, looked at the sea of dark faces and asked, 'Anyone in this carriage speak English?' A very old Thursday Island lady replied sharply 'What do you think, we speaking bloody Japanese already.'[47]

The destination for the McGinness and Kruger families in South Australia was Balaklava, a country town 92 kilometres north of Adelaide. The Balaklava Showgrounds were offered to the evacuees because the South Australian Premier, Thomas Playford advised Prime Minster Curtin that 'it was impossible to billet coloured persons with families.'[48] Their first accommodation there was at the town racetrack. There were a number of Darwin families at Balaklava. They included the Rivers, Fejo's and Batcho's. Bob McCoy was the protector of Aborigines stationed in Balaklava. A number of the families were accommodated on local farms. Jack McGinness's family and the Krugers rented Cottle's farm.

---

46 Ogden, *Katherine's Wartime Years*, 4.
47 Ogden, *Women of Katherine*, 88.
48 Ogden, *Women of Katherine*, 87.

Jungung

Katherine Railway workshops and yards during World War II. (Unknown, NTL, Alexander Fleetwood Collection, PH0546-0023).

With his family safe in South Australia Jack McGinness continued working on the railway during a period of extraordinary activity in Katherine. The railway was essential to Australia's war effort as a means of transporting military personnel and supplies to and from Darwin. Following the Bombing of Darwin the Army took control of the North Australia Railway on 23 February 1942. Its main workshops were moved from Darwin to Katherine which became the main railway maintenance centre from Birdum to Adelaide River and operated 24 hours a day. A spur line from the main track was constructed across the main street (now Katherine Terraces) to a site running along the riverbank from First to Fourth Street. New workshops and railway yards were established.[49]

After the evacuation of most of the civilian population in 1942, those who remained in Katherine, store owners, local essential services, railway workers and farmers, contributed to the military in some way. Katherine had become a military town and was transformed by the extent of the military presence. Up to 150 military units and detachments passed through Katherine during the war. Although some combat units used Katherine as a base most were service units. These carried out the full gamut of military functions including pay, canteen, censorship, butcher, postal detachments, supply and transport, signals, dispatch riders, cipher and telegraph, dental services, malaria control laboratories, major hospital, military police, security details, headquarters units and railway construction and movement companies.[50]

---

49   Ogden, *Katherine's Wartime Years*, 8.
50   Reed & Croft, *The Fall of the Daisy Cutters*, 23.

Little is known of Jack's time during the war. One thing that did not change was that Jack continued to befriend and help others. These friendships continued for life and changed the family forever. Kathy remembers this of George Cummings.

> George Cummings was a young drover from Lake Nash and Alexandra Downs Station near the Queensland border. He first met Jack in 1942 while droving a herd of cattle on the journey to Wyndham in WA which ended at Mataranka in the NT. One possible explanation is that they would truck the cattle by rail direct to Darwin instead of droving the herd to Wyndham. George found himself stranded without a job which threatened his independent spirit so he started looking for work. He was introduced to Jack who at the time was standing in for the road master which subsequently took him to Mataranka a small railway siding 100 kms south of Katherine. George, being born and bred in and around the cattle industry, didn't know the first thing about railway work. He needed a job and approached Jack for a job on the railway. Having a very strong work ethic and being eager to learn was enough for Jack to offer him a job as a fettler on the Mataranka gang under the guidance of George Holtze. George and the other Holtze men were also stock and cattlemen/fettlers for the North Australian Railways so Cummings was left in good company. This was the turning point for George Cummings as he never went back to droving, he more or less broadened his experience as a freelancer. He worked as a council worker in Alice Springs and Tennant Creek before taking up work as a winch driver for Noble's Nobb mine and spent some time with the Warrego and Peko mine before returning to Katherine in 1948. Wherever he went, whether it was in Tennant Creek or Darwin, he started a garden and he became very well known for his knack in growing Chinese cabbage and tomatoes. After a short stay in Katherine he transferred to Darwin where he settled and worked as the ganger of the section of line called 22 Mile, now the Wishart Siding under the Heritage of the Northern Territory. George could not read or write but he was still able to satisfy and carry out his duties as a ganger with what he was taught. I married David Mills, George's step son, and David worked there as well. It was during this period that George revealed to me that he had the highest regard for Jack for giving him a start on the railway when he was a young man right back in 1942. He said, "Jack McGinness showed me how to make hard work easy"

The McGinness family remained in Balaklava for about three years. The McGinness and Kruger women and children stayed together the whole time until their return to their beloved Katherine. *Ulñyunduboo* had also joined them. They shared a farm cottage owned by the Cottle family at Saints Siding on the way to Bowmans. The local farmers were German families, the Voigts, Boans, Coles and Scythes, who let their farm houses out for the evacuees. Kathy remembers the time in Balaklava as being good because the family was able to stay together.

Jungung

Although it was not an easy life, some lifelong friendships were made. Although the Cottle family were their landlords they shared some of their farm produce with their Darwin tenants. The older girls Joyce and Violet helped with some of the jobs on the farm. They had to adapt to the colder climate and they relied on coupons for food and essentials. The children walked to school. The school itself was housed in a farm barn. The evacuee community was kept separate from the Balaklava community.[51]

School at Balaklava, April 1943. (Unknown, Mills Collection).

To help the war effort the Red Cross would drop off bundles of wool for women to knit socks and scarves to be sent overseas to the Australian troops. Violet, Lily and Lucy were involved in the exercise as were the older girls. Joyce became an expert knitter in later years probably due to that earlier experience.

Jack McGinness was able to visit his family in Balaklava during his rest and recreation leave although it is not clear just how many visits he was able to make. Kathy has fond memories of those times and family trips into Balaklava. The family would visit Violet's cousin Martha Serano and other NT evacuees such as the Russell family, Aunty Rhoda, the Stew family of Juana Calma and Norm Youram. There were also visits to Peterborough where other Darwin evacuees were living. Aunty Ada Ah Matt's family was there as were the Evans. Kathy also

---

51   Mills, Kathy, Oral History Interview, NTRS 3163 BWF 25_S2_2.

recalls one occasion when he took the family to Semaphore beach in Adelaide where there was a fun fair. Kathy had never seen a merry go round with its bucking horses and some other fair attractions.[52] There were was also special memories of a lunch at the Terminus Hotel in Balaklava.

Terminus Hotel, Balaklava. (Mills Collection).

On another occasion Dad took Sadie and Kathy into Adelaide and we stopped at the Peoples Palace run by the Salvation Army. The excitement of the 'big smoke' and a young boy on crutches selling newspapers and calling 'Hindley Street tripple murderrrr, three men dead in city firrre' was an adventure never to be forgotten. Among the throngs of people and above all the clamour of traffic and hustle bustle there was a familiar voice calling "Jack McGinness!" We were so surprised to find a woman from Katherine, Mrs Lya Topmakoff, who was very close to our family and grateful that Jack and Violet cared for her children when she needed to go away for medical treatment.

As the tide of War turned in favour of the Allied forces it was decided at the Commonwealth Inter-departmental Conference held in Melbourne in February 1945, that the lifting of the Northern Territory Emergency Control Regulations that would enable civilians to return to their homes should take place in two stages. First the area south of Pine Creek and secondly the area north of Pine

---

52 Mills, Kathy, Oral History Interview, NTRS 3163 BWF 25_S2_2.

Jungung

Creek.⁵³ This meant that after three years in Balaklava the McGinness family could return to Katherine in mid 1945.

For families to return they needed to prove to the authorities that they had accommodation to live in. Jack McGinness could bring his family home because he had a house to bring them home to. George Kruger had property but he did not have a house built on it so he and Putt Ah Matt, who was married to George's step sister Ada Gibbs, decided to bring their families home - the deal being that they build two houses on George's block, one for the Kruger family and the other for Ada and Putt Ah Matt. The team of Jack McGinness, George and the Ah Matt men, Putt, John, and Jaffa set about to build the two houses so both families could return home. Other Katherine pre-war families to return included the Hunt's, Forscutt's, Rawl's, McLeane's, Beer's and Kruger's.

The town had changed a great deal during the war. There were more people and more buildings. The military had constructed many new buildings during the war years. The Sydney Williams huts were everywhere in the town. The McGinness house had been used for recreation purposes during the war and as a result the family inherited a piano which had been left there when the troops departed. Jack McGinness remained in Katherine working for the railways under the control of the Manpower during the war. Although the family home had been commandeered by Manpower, Jack was able to keep an eye on it. Life returned to normal after the war fairly quickly. The Katherine school reopened with a former serviceman, John Lucas as the teacher. Some of Katherine's pre-war institutions also returned. Cox's store was Katherine's only shop and as such provided an essential service to the town.⁵⁴

Katherine School, c1940s. (Unknown, NTL, Herbert Wong Collection, PH0433-0029).

---

53 Ogden, *Katherine's Wartime Years*, 25.
54 Mills, Kathy, Oral History Interview, NTRS 3163_26_3_1.

World War II

Picture theatre in wartime, c1943. Eventually this became Jack Neal's theatre which was operational about 1947-48. (Unknown, NTL, Henry & Gwen Scott Collection, PH0663-0131).

The women of Katherine played an important role in re-establishing community life in the town. In the event of any social occasion it was the women who prepared the hall and prepared the food for others to enjoy. Dances were popular events at the time. The mainstays of the Katherine band at the time were Scotty McLean on the drums and Mrs Scott who played the piano and sang. Many others joined the band when they could. Katherine also had a theatre left over from the war where films were shown but also musical theatrical performances were held. The remaining troops in the town and the community got on well together.

The end of the war was celebrated in Katherine. There was a fancy dress ball and Kathy Mills was dressed as 'Miss Victory'. Mrs Ivanich was part of Katherine's pre war Russian community dressed her children as the King and Queen of Peanuts. Mrs Smyth was the sewing and religious instruction teacher at school and organised the tennis club. Mrs Timble was a dress maker as was Mrs Love who in the absence of stores provided an important service to the town.[55]

At the end of the war the military presence in Katherine reduced quickly but it was replaced by the men of the Allied Works Council (AWC) or Civil Construction Corp (CCC) which took on the task of rebuilding Katherine. They repaired

---

55   Mills, Kathy, Oral History Interview, NTRS 3163_26_3_1.

Jungung

buildings and infrastructure for civilian use. The CCC included Harry Vallence, a pre-war Victorian Football League football star. We later found that Harry is regarded as a legend in Aussie Rules in Melbourne, which probably attracted him to Jack for his interest in Aussie Rules and involvement in the local competition.[56] In 1975 after Cyclone Tracy, Jack's daughter Sadie and her husband Vic Ludwig contacted and visited Harry and his wife Lorna in North Brighton where they lived. They found that he was known as Soapy and to their total amazement as they recall seeing the numerous trophies he had won. There was literally a stash of trophies and memorabilia stored in a shed behind the house. Vic said that he was amazed at what he saw and said that he had never seen or known of any footballer who had so many trophies. Harry very kindly gave Sadie and Vic this autographed photo of himself as a memento of their visit which is kept and treasured. Vic Ludwig is also a legend when it comes to football in Darwin as the longest serving President of any football team. His unbroken record of service to the Saint Mary's Football Club spans from the inception into the Darwin Football League in 1952 until 2004.

Soapy Valance in full flight.
(Unknown, Mills Collection).

---

56 Henry Francis 'Soapy' Vallence is a true legend of the Carlton Football Club, and one of the most prolific goal scorers of all time. In a stellar 204 game VFL career between 1926 and 1938, he kicked 722 goals. http://www.blueseum.org.

The CCC disbanded in 1946 but a number of the men decided to stay on in Katherine after their duties came to an end.[57] Jack McGinness continued with the railway throughout this period while his wife worked in the hospital laundry providing washing and ironing services to the Army nurses.

The war was responsible for the breakup of many families who were the other casualties of the war and the McGinness family was no exception. The effects of separation, lifestyle adjustment and the different approach to survival proved too great for many families and there was no turning back. Jack and Violet's lives had changed forever and the interruption caused by the war was devastating. Not having the time to readjust to their previous way of life, their marriage was in tatters. They eventually separated with Violet moving out to rent a small house owned by Bob Winton that was vacated by Old Charlie Arab and Jack left the railways and moved to Darwin. Violet remained in Katherine until her death, aged forty five, on 7 October 1954.[58]

Bond's Tours' bus in front of Katherine Hotel, on the main road in Katherine, NT, c1947. (Harris, K., SLSA, Album Collection, B 70782/37).

---

57 Northern Territory Library, *Military Units Index*.
58 *NS*, 14 October 1954.

Jungung

Katherine debutantes ball, c1952. Back row L-R: Unknown, June Mahoney, Kathy Mills, Nilla Ivanitz, Kathy Tutty Faye Dodson. Front row: Deidre Mahoney, Janie Smythe, Jennie McPherson, Gwynne Kennedy, Denise Mahoney. (Unknown, Mills Collection).

World War II

Darwin, 1945. (Image courtesy NT Department of Infrastructure, Planning and Logistics © Northern Territory of Australia).

Chapter 7

Post World War II: The Fight for Rights

My biggest recollection is when I worked with him. I didn't work, I was accompanying him in those days, but I suppose I was learning all the time too, how difficult it was for him, because he would get the reputation as a stirrer, and the name that was back there was that 'ratbag'. Today, it's called 'activist'.

But if you were deemed to be a ratbag, back there, you were a person of suspicious character. You would be seen as treasonous, plotting against the Government. We couldn't, mind you, sit around, a group of Aboriginal people in a house, because it would look like a conspiracy, and they could come and break you up and say: 'You mob go back to your own home now. Where do you live, and who are you?' And just walk in and question you. You couldn't have a group of people in your home. Yeah, that was such at the time.

So, I suppose I keep on reinforcing what I feel was the driving point for Dad to do that. Then, I was very, very proud when they ran him as the President of the North Australian Workers' Union. And I stand to be challenged, but I think he might be the first Aboriginal person to be a President of any trade labor union in Australia.[59]

The post-World War II period was one of reconstruction and the revival of pre-war action of asserting human rights affecting part Aboriginal people.

After his marriage breakup and his eventual move to Darwin, Jack worked a short time as a truck driver for his son in law Jim Stanton and partner Boyne Litchfield. Not too long after he landed a job with the carpentry section of the Department of Works and Housing. He was then promoted to leading hand bridge carpenter in charge of the reconstruction of the Stokes Hill Wharf, which was bombed during the war.

> During this period, he met Vic Ludwig, who was to marry Jack's daughter, Sadie. "He was a very impressive man that people could relate to or look up to, as a leader," said Vic. "I think you could safely say that Jack was a born leader. People have that knack in life, and some people don't. Some people want to be leaders but can't, and others can do it like falling off a log. It just comes so easy to them because they just have that charisma about them, I guess, to be leaders.

---

59 Mills, Kathy, Personal communication with Matthew Stephen, 24 May 2019. Kathy could not recall where this quote was originally documented.

"And when people go asking someone for advice on how to do things, and regardless of whether he was black or white, or Chinese, or whatever, you got that feeling that Jack had that. He just had that charisma about him."[60]

"He probably had a gang of probably twenty people, and they were all colours and creeds. But Jack had the sort of authority that people listen to. I never heard of anyone that couldn't work with Jack, or wouldn't work with Jack. So, yeah, he always had that something about him."[61]

The Town Yard Gang and the Rebirth of Darwin's Community.

The works depot was called the Town Yard. It was situated in Darwin on the corner block of McMinn and Bennett Street opposite Hornibrooks, and was the dry dock for small wooden crafts such as boat luggers, rafts etc. The caretaker at the time was Alan McGuire. Alan was a local who lived for many years in Darwin and one time umpire for Aussie rules mentioned in an earlier chapter. My husband David Mills and I would visit Alan on occasions when David was visiting his special cultural place in the Dinah Beach area. We would call in to Alan in his little caravan as he was one of the few people remaining in Darwin who remembered David's father Rupert Mills, a local *Larrakia* Man. Hornibrooks was a small stretch of pebble beach in the Francis Bay port area opposite the Town Yard Depot and adjacent to the Railway Station.

The Town Yard gang consisted of Jack, Tom D'Antoine, Bill Muir, Victor Raymond and a Yugoslav man whose name I do not recall and other temporaries. The corker in the gang was Tom D'Antoine who came from Broome, Western Australia. The job of the corker was to repair any vessels that may have sprung leaks and generally keep the vessel watertight and replace any planks that might have been damaged. Billy Muir was offsider to Jack and Victor Raymond was offsider to Tom D'Antoine. Jack remained with the Works and Jerks as it was called, from then until his retirement.

Bill Muir's wife Hilda, an *Alawa* woman from Booroloola, recalls how as a young 16 year old trainee nurse in Katherine she first met Jack McGinness and his wife Violet. She was given the opportunity to train by the Chief Protector Dr Cecil Cook who was responsible for setting up many training positions for Aboriginal people who were placed in Kahlin Compound in Darwin. She had been introduced to the McGinness couple by her colleague Daisy Ruddick who was a relative of Violet. Daisy was also a young trainee nurse under the guidance of Doctor Cook. Hilda remembers the support and guidance she received from the couple at a crucial

---

60 Ludwig, Vic, *Oral History Interview by Di Koser*, 5.
61 Ludwig, Vic, *Oral History Interview by Di Koser*, 4.

part of her life having no direct family around to turn to. She remains very close to the McGinness family and both Jack and Violet took interest in her while she trained in Katherine. In later years Hilda remembered that Jack would sometimes "growl at her dear old husband Bill" as she put it. Jack was the leading hand in charge at the town yard depot where Bill Muir worked. Bill and the other younger members regarded him as their mentor and father figure and respected him as their ganger in charge.

Victor Raymond came from Thursday Island and his experience working as a deep-sea diver suited him for the job of corking and replacing damaged planks. The reconstruction of Stokes Hill Wharf was the main objective of this jolly band of workers under the supervision of the Department of Works and Housing who provided the various Engineers for the project

Bob Henness, an acquaintance of Jack, met Mim McGinness at a Labor Party gathering and it was found that Bob got to know Jack when he was young man and employed as an electrician with the North Australian Railways. Bob recalls that Jack was working on the reconstruction of the Stokes Hill Wharf when they first met and later when Jack returned to the railways and was stationed at the 22 Mile fettler camp. Jack was recalled to extend the rail track onto the Wharf. Bob was a member of the ALP involved in the union movement at the time Jack was nominated as President of the NAWU.[62]

At the time Bob worked there, Allen Smith's father was working as a crane driver and his job was loading and unloading cargo on and off the goods train at Hornibrooks. Bob recalls Smith built the shop off the Stuart Highway at the 18 Mile on Virginia road, which held a gallon license. Other identities working for the NAR were Hallet, who was the cargo checker, James Grant, store man, Bill Keelan, the station master and Big Jaffa Ah Matt who was the Shunter for the trains. Two Malayan/Asian men also part of the Gang were Talum, who lived in a hut against Railway Hill and Homer Kanango, who had helped the army in the Philippines. Talum was known as the cat man because he would fish in his spare time and dry the fish. All the unused fish fed the town cats and there were literally dozens of them when Talum returned. Bob reflects on his time with Jack as a man of great knowledge, whether it was debating the political front, the Buffalo Football Club or wind direction. Bob felt inspired and encouraged by him.

---

62 Jack McGuinness, NAWU President, 1955-58, 1962-63, Brian, B., *One Big Union*, 294.

Post World War II: The Fight for Rights

Allan Smith first met Jack when Alan's father worked for the railways at the Town terminus next to where Jack worked at the Town Yard.[63] A glimpse into the diversity of the post-war community apparently impacted on a young Allan as he has since set his own agenda and political pathway. He has developed a profile as an industrious worker in the development of sport in the rural area and is to be recognized as a campaigner for worthwhile causes some of which require extreme personal effort. His brother Kelvin Gardiner had a brick works business in Mitchell Street behind Heavens shoe store, next door to where Jack lived in Mitchell Street.

The other neighbours were Fred and Eileen Laughton. Fred was a retired service man and worked for the Darwin Town Council while Jack worked for Department of Works and Housing. As well as being neighbours both men had mutual respect for each other, Fred as a defender of human rights in uniform, while Jack was a defender of Rights in civvies. Fred being a man of quiet patience admired Jack for his ability to speak out on community issues or matters of concern to Aboriginal Affairs. Fred was a staunch supporter of the Union, a quiet achiever and Jack had admiration for Fred because he was a war veteran which Jack regretted not having had the opportunity to serve his country in that respect. The Laughton's, like so many Aboriginal families around Australia, served in the armed forces and this became part of the family tradition. Fred, Allan and Herbert senior, served in the first medical trials for malaria and dengue fever while work was being carried out on new serums and antidotes during World War II. Herbert although having a disability was attached to the Medical Corp researching tropical medicine for malaria and dengue fever. Herbert's son Kenny later continued the family tradition of military service in the Vietnam War.[64]

---

63 Allan Smith expressed his willingness to speak at the launch of this book when it was first in development in 2004. On behalf of my father Jack I wish to thank Allan for his offer.
64 Bray, Laughton & Foster, *Aboriginal Ex-Servicemen of Central Australia*, 8-13.

Jungung

Eileen and Fred Laughton. Neighbours in Mitchell St, c 1950s.
(Unknown, Mills Collection).

Kelvin Gardiner was self-employed and was involved in industrial affairs with other union groups as well as the Waterside Workers. The waterside workers featured very strongly in supporting the FAACTSI movement in Queensland and the Eastern Seaboard which emerged during the late 1950s.

Mitchell Street and the top end of Smith Street was developing as the post-war commercial area with the Post Office on one side of the street and the paper shop down the street on the other side. On the opposite side was the Magistrate's Court of petty sessions.

The community around Mitchell Street was typical of a town rebuilding and the political climate was interesting to say the least. There were groups of vacant Sydney William Huts in that area after the war which fledgling businesses were quick to take advantage of. Most of the abandoned Army huts around Darwin became important for housing the community as well as striving business houses. The business community was heavily involved in the rebuilding of post-war Darwin and their efforts are to be recognised as some continue in business houses today. They developed their own rebuilding campaign by planting tropical plants around the huts using the abandoned rims, bomb racks and tank tracks to attract customers and beautify the sombre landscape left by Darwin's military occupation during World War II. When financial stability returned some businesses moved to other premises while others took their place. Through the re-growth of the business world, the local economy began to stabilise.

The hut occupied by the Registry Office was later used by Shombachers who started a dress shop and music store opposite to Les Heavens' shoe store. Humour became part and parcel of post-war Darwin and proprietor Les Heavens stole the show with the quip above his store "Send your soles to Heavens". There developed a unique humour and community spirit and other traders followed in the satire, some of which cannot be written down but spend some time with the old timers and they may share the stories with you. The humour continued well after the initial rebuilding. Millers and Sandovers, a hardware store in Smith Street, was referred to as Killers and Standovers, while Jolly's general store on Woolworth block was called "Not so jolly". Wog Alley was the walkway along the side of the Greek Club that led from Smith Street to Mitchell Street and Rocky's Park. Social etiquette does not permit such terminology in these days of racial vilification laws, but it was freely spoken in Darwin and was not intended as a slur. Many well known members of the Greek Community were involved in the club and it served as a community centre rather than an exclusive club. Respectability was a political issue as was everything else in the re-growth of Darwin and it wasn't long before changes were made to alter attitudes and common talk.

The only terminology with racial connotations that appears to have been sanctioned is China Town. It was the section of town around Cavenagh Street where Chinese Merchants and traders carried out their business in pre-war Darwin. The area known as Malay town and Japanese and Philippine quarters did not survive in post-war Darwin. China Town remains as a historical heritage area and was also used to promote a development in Mitchell Street in recognition of the contribution made by the Chinese People in the business world of Darwin.

Cavenagh Street, Chinatown, c1938. (Unknown, NTAS, HSNT Collection, NTRS 1854 Item 376).

Jungung

The union movement which Jack was involved in was very active with the return to civil construction work after the war time contribution of Manpower.[65] Local issues concerning workers' rights included the lack of housing which became very much a part of their mandate and a very busy and progressive time it was. Jack was living in a shed on Jim Stanton's block before he moved to a disused building at Bullocky Point. The house was the property of the Vesteys' meatworks that had been abandoned after the war. The adjoining building was occupied by Jim and Nell Richards who ran the DX Bakery, the only local supplier at the time. Nell was the daughter of Bob Murray, a patron of the early Buffalo Football Club, and a personal friend of Jack. Jim and Nell were strong supporters of the Union and they supported the apprenticeship board.

David Mills and William Fejo were the first baker's assistants to be trained under the development scheme after the war. Bill Alcorn was a private contractor and he supplied the firewood for the bakery. Bill also needed workers for his contract and offered anyone the opportunity to cut firewood. David took up wood-cutting for a short time but contract work had not developed any working conditions that were attractive to young men and David went in search for other work.

Other men working for Bill Alcorn were Nugget Blackmore and Bill Goodall who worked the Rapid Creek area and along the RAAF fence. Felling the trees for firewood around the fence line also provided a fire break. Their accommodation was a canvas tarpaulin strung between four saplings and a cyclone bed with a mosquito net if you were lucky. Housing was poor for anyone at the time but what the union was concerned about was the fact there was no plan to cater for workers. Housing was only offered to southern recruits as an incentive and to attract skilled workers involved in Administration necessary for the rebuilding of Darwin. The local laborers did not have any entitlements to government housing and were responsible for their own accommodation needs. Abandoned houses and sheds became the usual for accommodation and the working men tolerated the situation to a point and then began to demand better consideration.

Part-Aboriginal people returning to Darwin were confined to a disused Army camp in Stuart Park, Camp 118 off Westralia Street and K9 Camp off Charles Street down from Francis Camp. Francis Camp housed single working men. Working as a member of the Trade Union Movement with the North Australian Workers Union, Jack lobbied for housing for labourers. Jack and Babe Basil Damaso were the first Aboriginal workers to be housed in what was called Administration

---

65 In 1942 the Manpower Directorate was established which took over responsibility for the *List of reserved occupations*. Generally the men who worked in these reserved occupations in the Northern Territory were referred to as Manpower. https://www.awm.gov.au.

Housing in the new development area of Fannie Bay. This led to Welfare providing some housing in the Ludmilla area before the Housing Commission developed.

The other issue that captured Jack's interest was the situation of young people. The teenage boys who were school leavers had literally nowhere to go once they left school. He became involved in the Apprenticeship Board that was being set up believing that "if a young man did a man's job he should be eligible for a man's pay". Don Bonson was another staunch supporter of the apprenticeship board as his sons and other young Aboriginal youths had completed the high school certificate. Further education was not available in Darwin and interstate boarding was out of reach for large families. Don became very active in the Union and the Apprenticeship board as a means to provide employment opportunity for his sons. There were other personal issues concerning his identity that caused Don much heartache which he became very passionate about.

Jack McGinness, c 1950s.
(Unknown, Mills Collection).

Taking up the Post-war Challenge of Workers' Rights and Housing

With the war over and as the Darwin community rebuilt with the return of old residents and the influx of new residents it was a period when old union issues resurfaced and threatened to undermine workers' rights, which led to Jack getting involved once more. The 1950's was a period when the political chapter to Jack's life was in full swing with the Trades and Labor movement, the Half Caste Progressive Association, and later as the President of the North Australian Workers Union.

Jack's involvement in the union movement since the mid-1920s gave him a great deal of experience in organising and speaking on behalf of others. He was always at the forefront of community activism to improve their living and working conditions. The strategic outcome of this activity was the reformation of The Half-caste Progressive Association in early 1951. Jack was elected the President of the re-formed Association.[66] The Association held regular formal meetings to address their objectives which were of a social and compassionate nature and well within the charter of advancing the position of Aboriginal people in society. This served as an opportunity to gather and discuss other matters of importance and remain legal. The unions supported the Half-caste Progressive Association by holding union meetings as well. Most of the Association members were members of the unions anyway, so it was difficult to isolate the political from the social.

All social events were held in the parish hall in Stuart Park, at ex-Army Camp 118 Parap, which was allocated for housing part-Aboriginal people after the war. Parap 118 Camp was the post war Half-caste quarters while Bagot Settlement was the Reserve Compound to house Full-bloods, the term that described the native people. Any contact with people outside these regimes was made very difficult and discouraged by the Authorities. The only contact with our people who were housed in reserves was through the control of the Native Affairs. Permits had to be applied for and validated with a stamped approval before any entry to the reserve was permitted. The permit was supplied with very strong directions specifying the persons identified and the time of the visit stipulated. Half-castes were also subject to the co-habitation law and strict control was applied.

---

66   The Northern Territory Half-Caste Progressive Association was formed in 1936 but its activities largely ceased during World War II. The Association was reformed in approximately 1951. See *CA*, 13 April 1951.

Joan McGinness (Angeles) doing the Hula
at sunshine Club, c1950s.
(Unknown, Mills Collection).

The association held dances and social events such as fetes for the purpose of fundraising which had to be seen as in keeping with the guidelines and objectives of Associations. Boxing nights were also arranged and supported by Tim Angeles, Dick Butler and other members of the community. The Police Boys club run by Bill Jacobs hosted a Boxing Troupe called the Kiwi Club which offered a welcome competition whose trainer was Terry Alderton. Boxing fans will recall some of the identities of the boxing fraternity: Koolpinya Kid (Jock Cassidy), Blacky (Simon Serano), Kanga Kid (Manny Talbot), Witjity (Jimmy Fejo), Eddie and Vincent Roe, Bobby Cadell ,Timmy Angeles, Lionel Butler and Johnny Hunter to mention a few.

Jungung

The people of mixed race in Camp 118 rallied to support the social events that occurred there and it became known as The Sunshine Club. Weddings and other social and personal functions were held at the Club and many great memories remain of the era. Social restrictions limited social interaction in the wider community and had it not been for the formation of the Sunshine Club the Aboriginal population would have endured a very dull existence. The musicians living in Camp 118 were restricted from playing in the local bands and playing at the Sunshine Club provided them the opportunity to express their talents for the people's pleasure. Discrimination by forced restrictions against the coloured people prevented them from playing with the existing band which was sponsored by the wife of the Administrator.

There was virtually an unlimited range of talent among the community 118 Parap Camp from musicians to singers, comedians and dancers. The band was open to any musician who offered their time and consisted of piano, drums, violin, steel guitar, mandolin, bush-base and banjo. Steve Abala, Peter Cardona and Jaffa Ah Matt played the steel guitar as well as rhythm and Jaffa was a maestro with the mandolin. Piano players included Steve Abala's sister Rowena Stroud, Clive Dowling, Margaret Perez, Sylvia Evans (Cheedles), Phillip Baban, and Simon Serrano. As interest grew the club attracted other musicians such as Nichols, who played the drums, and Div Collinson (saxophone) who added to the sound.

Mildred (Mim) McGinness & Cecilia Muir at the Sunshine Club, c1950s.
(Unknown, Mills Collection).

One of the most memorable events was entering a float in the Labor Day March in 1951. A yearly competition was held to choose a May Queen for the Labor Day March and the AHPA entered a float to advertise the Association and its aims. The event served as a debut to society, the float was beautifully decorated and took full part in the parade. Dawn Cooper was the AHPA May Queen and supported by maids in waiting Margaret Angeles and Kathleen McGinness. The AHPA under the leadership of Jack McGinness broke down many barriers and boosted the morale of all who worked with him. The people who worked with Jack were very dedicated. Elna and Tim Angeles, Babe Damaso, Monica Lew Fatt, Joe and Daisy Ruddick were just a few of the dedicated staff.

Citizenship Rights

During Jack's time in the NAWU, the union was gearing up to address the treatment of Aboriginal people in the Territory and take it all the way to Federal level through arbitration. There was two main union groups, the North Australian Workers Union and the Federation of Waterside Workers. Although they were meeting to address their own political platforms however they both joined forces to address the Aboriginal issue and delegates from each Union attended the meetings of the AHPA.

The Aboriginal population was dissected by law and classified as the Half-caste or mixed race and the Full-blood, meaning those Aboriginal people whose pigmentation was intact. Fathers of part aboriginal children made up a substantial number of the membership and a very ambitious and vocal group it was. Joe Ruddick, Ian Jamison and Yorki Peel were the most outspoken. They were there to protect the interest of their mixed blood children. The importance of having an identity was raised and the call for support to identify their children as Eurasian was the platform for their cause. The word was a combination of European Australian and Asian which specified the regional global position of Australia. This was to establish their origin of birth and their identification as a distinct group with distinct rights. Classification as it stood then was determined by the pigmentation of their skin, which classified them as a distinct group but without distinct rights or any other rights for that matter. They could be removed from the care and control of their parents if so decided by the authorities in power whose right of removal could be enforced by the Assimilation Policy.

There were other suggestions of identity put forward, but to adopt a new classification would seem to confuse the main issue and perhaps weaken the position of what was already being presented. Not taking the issue forward does not suggest that the issue was defeated but deferred for a later time in the struggle.

Jungung

Removal of existing legislative laws that disempowered and discriminated against Aboriginal people was the main issue at the time. This meant the recognition of full citizen rights for all Aboriginal people irrespective of the colour of their skin.

A most disturbing incident surrounding Jack's family and his son-in-law's failed attempt to have an uncle who came from Wave Hill Station visit with the family. The reason why the uncle was brought to Darwin was not known to the family but knowing he was in town prompted them to go to Bagot Compound and request he visit the family. Jim thought that it was just a matter of going and picking him up and then taking him to their home in Stuart Park. Access was denied due to regulations that controlled and restricted movement of Aboriginal people of full blood descent.

Proof was required that the dwelling that he was to visit had a separate ablution block before approval was granted. The suggestion was highly insulting. Efforts to resolve the problem were rejected and an argument ensued, "a row as big as a fight", as Jack would say. The point was made that the status of his wife's independence was questionable under the Act. Violet was not an exempted person, which Jim was not aware of. The incident was used in Jack's address to the ACTU Congress in Melbourne and pointed out as being an example of the ridiculous nature of *The Act* controlling Aboriginal people. Jack could draw from a long list of experiences to put to Congress but he viewed the incident with his family as the ultimate insult and an example of the extreme inhumane action taken against people. As it stood, his son-in-law could go for an evening stroll but his wife and children were restricted from accompanying him.

The union movement around Australia was stirring and gaining momentum and two major political parties with vigorous platforms were in full flight. Both platforms added fuel to the causes, to promote and re-establish post-war worker's rights and to support the national movement for recognition of Human Rights for Aboriginal people of Australia.

> The unions decided to back the association, because Jack was a very prominent unionist. And they sent him down south to Melbourne, to a huge union conference. He was to speak at that meeting on the matter of ordinary, part-Aboriginal people having to be under the Aboriginal Act, when they were living lives of ordinary citizens, doing very well at all sorts of jobs.

> And a large number of these people had been overseas, fighting for supposedly their country, to come back and find out that they weren't allowed into town after dark, and various other little things —the wives couldn't get the baby bonus or the child endowment. So it was a very difficult time for these people.

> And I was given the job of getting exemptions for these people. Jack was very busy with getting as much information and sending deputies and all sorts of various things to the Administrator at the time—and working with the union. And I felt, always, that Jack was a very - a man, you know, that was looking into the future. He was thinking about things that other people weren't even interested in at the time.[67]

Jack was elected in July 1951 to attend the Australian Council of Trade Union (ACTU) Congress in Melbourne in September. It was seen as a historic decision as 'the first time that a representative of N.T. half-castes has attended the congress.' Jack made his intentions for his participation at the Congress clear. The objective of the Half Caste Progressive Association was to gain full citizenship rights for half-castes. 'With full A.C.T.U. backing we may achieve our aims and get rid of the dog collar system. We have been wearing dog collars all or lives.' For good measure Jack also called on the Commonwealth Minister for Territories, Paul Hasluck, to consider appointing a part Aboriginal to the Legislative Council as had been recently done in Papua New Guinea.[68]

Jack and other Aboriginal statesmen from around Australia realised that they had no control over their lives and no rights to claim their own land or their inherent rights of either parent. The "Movement", The Aboriginal Advancement League, started in the early 30s' was rekindled. Unionists around Australia became very involved in what was called "The Struggle" and the Communist Party was bringing pressure to bear with their obvious support. Jack's involvement with the trade union movement and executive member of the North Australian Workers Union as well as President of the Half-caste Progress Association meant he was the appropriate delegate to represent the Territory at State Conferences.

Jack's attendance at the ACTU Congress in Melbourne was packed with events. One held in Fitzroy was headed by Paster Doug Nicholls and Bill Onus, President of the Australian Aborigines League.

> In silence, the little group heard Mr McGinness say exploitation of native labor in the N.T. was rife. Big cattle stations kept the natives on low wages without a chance of elevating themselves. The Native Affairs branch had done little to help natives. The natives wanted to learn trades, and become more than just rouse-abouts. They wanted a vote, and citizenship rights. Mr McGinness said half-castes were seeking the aid of the A.C.T.U. to obtain abolition of the ordinance, under which they were barred from a town between 5p.m. and 8a.m. unless they had a license.[69]

---

67 Clarke, Sheila, *Oral History Interview with Di Koser*, 2.
68 *NS*, 31 July 1951.
69 *The Age,* 30 August 1951.

Jungung

The meeting further called for Aboriginal self determination and recognition of Aboriginal culture.

Jack's attendance at the ACTU Congress in Melbourne was not all business. It gave him the opportunity to see his sister Margaret Edwards for the first time in 17 years.[70] Margaret moved to Melbourne with her husband Harry Edwards in 1933.[71] During that time she had become involved in Aboriginal issues and was able to introduce Jack to some of the most important Aboriginal activists of the time.[72] This included national representatives of the Aboriginal Advancement League where he exchanged information of what each state was doing. He established a lasting friendship with Sir Douglas Nicholls, Harold Blair, and Captain Reg Saunders who were very important men in their respective regions as well as many various others.

The Black Diggers as they were called on the battlefield were reduced to nobodies on their return to their country. Steve Abala (son of Barney McGuiness) and other Aboriginal service men were very actively vocal in that respect.[73] They marched in the ANZAC marches and engaged in the speeches that followed, telling listeners that they had the freedom to fight and die for their country but their country did not free them from their own bondage to live equally on their return. Once back on their native soil they were subject to the same regime that they left, that of the *Native Affairs Act*. There were no citizenship rights and Aboriginal people did not feature in the census. They were not able to go to a pub to enjoy a beer with their comrades. They deserved better and they were more determined than ever to change the rules.

Curfews were in place at that time which prevented after-hours meetings in individual homes. People were advised that the gatherings could be viewed as illegal. Rallies and meetings were held around Darwin under the watchful eye of the Native Affairs Welfare Department who sent an officer of the Department to each meeting to report on those who attended and the activities of the meetings.

70　The Argus, 30 August 1951.
71　Harry's trade declined as motorised transport became increasing popular, and so he and Margaret moved to Melbourne in 1933. Margaret became an active member of the Council for Aboriginal Rights (Victoria). http://ia.anu.edu.au.
72　Mills, Kathy, Personal communication with Matthew Stephen, 29 March 2019.
73　Egan, *The Role Models,* 6-7.

Post World War II: The Fight for Rights

Jack McGinness with his sister Margaret Edwards
in Melbourne. *Argus*, 30 August 1951

When the time came for Jack McGinness's address to the Congress he began nervously in front of what was probably the largest crowd he had ever seen.[74] Nevertheless it was a 'personal triumph' with union delegates who listened in silence to his speech and then 'cheered and clapped' at its conclusion 'calling for full citizenship rights for half-castes and improved living standards for full-bloods.'[75]

---

74 *The Argus*, 6 September 1951
75 The *Argus*, 8 September 1951.

Jungung

Jack McGinness addressing the Australian Council of Trade Union Congress, Melbourne, 1951.

Maritime Worker, Saturday 29 September 1951.

Address By Aboriginal Delegate Mr Jack McGinness To ACTU Congress

I propose to divide my address on the Aborigine Question into two portions.

1. The demand for full citizenship rights for part-Aborigines

2. The Aborigines, their right to survival as a race, their right to be treated as human beings and not as outcasts from the human family.

I will deal with the question of full citizenship rights from the Aborigines, because the approach and the solution to full citizenship rights is different to the full -blooded Aborigines as a whole.

We the part Aborigine, have an unjust ordinance imposed on us that is against the wishes of the people living in the Territory; it is against the wishes of every industrial, political, religious, cultural and sporting organisation in the Territory, and our demands were supported by every political candidate at the last federal elections. Mr Jock Nelson assured my organisation that it had the support of the Federal Labor Caucus, and full citizenship rights would be granted to us if the Labor Party were to return to power. Unfortunately for more than us, that did not happen.

Support Needed

My Union felt the best way in which this particular question could be presented to you for your support would be the personal attendance of a part Aborigine, unaccompanied by any other delegate, so that you could readily see there is no justification for withholding from us of what should be our inalienable right: the right to live as ordinary people, without segregation from the rest of the community. We are educated at the same schools, take our part in every sporting and industrial sphere on equal footing with other peoples of the Territory, but, because of the pigmentation of our skin is dark, and we have original Australians as part of our ancestry, we are classed as something that is tainted and must be kept apart. What reason or justification is there for such an attitude on the part of the Government of this country?

I will be speaking about how the Aborigine Ordinance affects me personally, but this effect applies to all others in the same category as myself. Possibly some of you know that, because we are of Aboriginal extraction, we are subject to, or come under the Aboriginal Ordinance, which states "That an Aboriginal or half caste can not remain in a town or prohibited area between the hours of 6 pm and 8 am, each day without a written permit, issued by the Director of Aboriginal Affairs." It rests with the individual whether you are entitled to a permit or not.

Movement Restricted

The Ordinance also states that no Aboriginal or Half Caste Aboriginal is permitted to enter or remain on any licensed premises without a certificate of exemption also issued by the Director of Native Affairs. This exemption also applies to people of only slight or, I may say, part Aborigines, where I can prove that it is impossible to trace any colour in them whatsoever. The only thing that will disclose their part Aboriginal blood is the records kept in the Native Affairs Office, where these people are classed as half castes.

In 1936, when the Native Affairs Department enforced these laws or ordinances, the half caste peoples formed an Association and applied for a general exemption from the said Ordinance. The Native Affairs Branch granted exemptions to selected members of the Association and, after a period, through the inactivity, the Association lapsed. Earlier this year, the Aboriginal Ordinance was enforced again and the Police Force became very active, and demanded to see a certificate of exemption from members of my Association before they were allowed to enter or stay on licensed premises. If the individual questioned could not produce the certificate, he was either ordered off the premises or escorted to the Police Station, and there charged with being in a prohibited area.

When I myself was approached by a Police Officer and asked to produce my exemption I informed him that I did not have it with me, that I did not think it necessary, as every hotel in the Territory had lists of names of all persons who were exempted under the Act. The publican was informed that I was not to be served with a drink and I was ordered off the premises. The policeman then went away and returned in a matter of two minutes or so, pulled out his notebeook, looked at it and said: "You have an exemption all right,but you cannot have another drink until you receive a certificate of exemption from the Director of Native Affairs, Mr. Moy."

Arising out of many incidents of a like nature, the Half Castes' Association was re-formed, with the attainment of full citizenship rights as our main objective. Resolutions were passed, and letters forwarded to our Federal Member and the Prime Minister, asking that our demands be met but to date nothing by the way of fulfilment has been achieved.

Further Anomalies

I am a married man with seven daughters and two sons. Four of my daughters were born before my wife and myself were exempted. They are classed as not exempted half castes but the other children are classed as exempted. What a farce. Brothers and sisters having a different classification. My second daughter married a white man and had two children before the authorities discovered she was an unexempted person. Under the Aboriginal Ordinance her husband is liable to arrest and prosecution for consorting with a female half caste Aboriginal, so, to avoid that, my son in law has to apply to the authorities for an exemption for his wife and two children. The absurd thing about the Ordinance is that the exemption covering a person can be revoked at any time. You can see gentlemen, that we are worse than foreigners in our own country.

With your assistance and solidarity of the Trade Union Movement we hope to bring our just and lawful demands to a successful conclusion. That is the reason I was delegated to come to this congress, place our case before you, and ask for your full support to achieve our aims, and give us the right to live as good citizens of this country, and as true Australians.

Now I will go on and deal with the second part of my address: The right of the Aborigines to survival as a race, and their right to be treated as human beings and not as outcasts from the human family.

Oppressed by States

Firstly, I would like to say that all Governments in Australia, both State and Federal, have neglected to face up to the problems that must be solved so that these peoples can be brought from their present stage of outcasts and slaves. And gentlemen, it is slavery that is imposed on these people.

They are not bound by chains to keep them in subjection, but they are prevented from receiving the education that is so necessary before they will be able to express their clear terms what is necessary for them to survive as a race. These people are classified as nomads because, in their native state, they are continually on the move. It is true they constantly travel from area to area, but that is not from choice, but sheer necessity. The native people were not kindly treated by nature when they were isolated on this continent now known as Australia. No native cereals indigenous to the country lend themselves to cultivation, no native fruits or vegetable exist that lend themselves to be produced for a stable community, and no native animals with the exception of the dingo can be domesticated. What was left to the Aborigine but the constant need to be a hunter and traveller that he can survive at all. This accident of nature prevented the Aborigine from becoming anything else but a nomad, and the generations that have succeeded generations it has become a part of the native way of life. It is something that cannot be eradicated overnight but must be dealt with sympathetically over a long period of time before the inner urge to travel is eradicated.

The actions of the stations, who are in the main the largest employers of native labor, encourage this wanderlust of the native. The seasons in the Territory are divided into two, the wet and dry. In the dry all work on the stations is done and the native supply is used up for this purpose. In the wet, the need for the native does not exist, so the station managers withdraw clothing that is issued to the natives during their useful working period. The natives are then told that when the wet season is over there will be work again, and they will get their clothing back again. The stations are not interested in the education of the native and make no attempt to provide any. An ignorant employee is an asset, but an educated one will not put up with the conditions.

Control of Aborigines in the Territory is vested in the Director of Native Affairs. As he was the individual directly responsible for the issue of the order that banished Fred Waters to Haast's Bluff, he has shown quite clearly that he is not a fit and proper person to administer a department that is supposed to show sympathy and understanding towards Aborigines.

No Easy Solution

Solution of the Native problem is not at all an easy one, but a solution can be found. Unfortunately through lack of education and knowledge of the white man's ways, the natives themselves have not been able to suggest the way that transition from the stone age to the present age can be brought about, but if the Commonwealth Government is imbued with a true intention to raise the Aborigine from his present standard, then a policy can be introduced that will preserve the Natives as an entity and prevent their eradication as a people.

And I recommend that the Australian Council of Trade Unions Congress ask the Commonwealth Government to abolish the Aboriginal Ordinances as apply to half caste and part Aborigine of the Northern Territory, and raise the full-blooded Aborigine from his present standard of living and introduce a policy that will preserve the Natives as entity and prevent their eradication as a people.

On the motion of Delegate T. [Tom] Wright, seconded by Secretary Broadby, the following resolution was carried:-

"Congress wholeheartedly supports and commends the request put forward to Congress by Mr. J. McGuinness, representing the North Australia Workers Union with reference to the plight of full Aborigines and half castes. These demands are considered by Congress to be the minimum necessary to allow these classes of people in the Australian community to be self respecting and to obtain a proper standard of living."

"Further, the Executive be directed to afford any assistance necessary to the N.A.W.U. to present the case of these classes of people before the belated inquiry to be conducted by the Commonwealth Government."

Post World War II: The Fight for Rights

When Jack returned to Darwin he immediately reported his experiences to the Half-caste Progressive Association. It was reported that his address to the ACTU Congress in Melbourne had resulted in an assurance not only 'of union support, but many independent bodies interested in helping their fellow men- irrespective of race and creed-' Furthermore it was seen that Jack's success at the Congress should act a catalyst to intensify the Half-Caste Progressive Association's campaign for 'full citizenship rights for all half-caste and part-aboriginal people.'[76]

The campaign for full citizenship rights achieved a major milestone in June 1953 when the *Aboriginal Ordinance* was replaced by the *Welfare Ordinance*. This liberated the Coloured community from the *Aboriginals Ordinance* by granting them citizenship but maintained other Aborigines as wards of the state. The hypocrisy of this "new deal" was that the Administration of the new *Ordinance* resulted in all but nine Northern Territory Aborigines being declared wards of the state.[77] For these Aboriginal 'wards', nothing had changed, they remained under the control of the Commonwealth Government and would do so until *Social Welfare Ordinance* abolished the concept of wardship in 1964. Jack's fight for rights would continue.

Union Leadership

Jack McGinness, 'Union Boss', *People*, 4 September 1957.

---

76   *NS*, 28 September 1951.
77   Tatz, 'Aboriginal Administration', 26.

In 1955 Jack McGinness was elected President of the North Australia Workers Union. As the first Aboriginal President of a major Australian Trade Union it was a historic achievement in both the Union movement and Indigenous rights. It had not been an easy path for Jack's election as President.

The 1950s was a period of increased optimism for the Northern Territory. The post war reconstruction and the buoyant cattle industry had lifted the Northern Territory economy and the hardships and austerity of the immediate post war period had eased. However, there were many social issues that needed to be addressed.

Jack McGinness's campaign for citizenship rights for Aborigines and his role at the 1951 ACTU Congress was a high point for the NAWU in its support for Aboriginal rights. During the 1950s the Union became embroiled in an increasingly bitter faction fight between its communist left and moderate right wings. Jack was very much in the middle of these tensions. Put in a nutshell the right-wing moderates saw the left faction as "disloyal' to the country and working for 'Joe Stalin', while the left wing depicted their opponents [on the right] as 'agents of Menzies'.[78]

The NAWU elections held in late 1951 Jack found himself on both the left and right wing's election tickets. Jack won the most votes for a position on the executive council.[79] In doing so he trod a difficult political line to successfully build alliances with both sides of the political divide. At the time, in the midst of the campaign for citizenship rights for Aborigines, he needed the support of the NAWU and he succeeded by gaining a position on the NAWU executive with the election of the right wing 'Democratic Team'.[80]

Jack's status in the Northern Territory community during this period was highlighted in 1953 when he was awarded one of 64 'Coronation Medals' granted in the Northern Territory as Australian Half-caste Progressive Association President and his role in the campaign for Aboriginal rights. Jack was celebrated along with Albert Namatjira, Aboriginal Artist and Jack White, discoverer of the Rum Jungle uranium deposit, as prominent Territorian recipients of Coronation Medals.[81]

The tensions between the left and right factions remained when Jack ran for NAWU President in 1955. The left faction again ran a ticket for every NAWU position but although they gained 25% of the vote the right prevailed with Jack elected as president with Baylon Ryan as secretary.[82] Although Jack had been on

---

78 *NS*, 18 May 1951. See also, Brian, Bernie., 'One Big Union', 239.
79 *NS*, 4 January 1952.
80 Brian, 'One Big Union', 242.
81 *NS*, 4 June 1953.
82 *NS*, 5 July 1955.

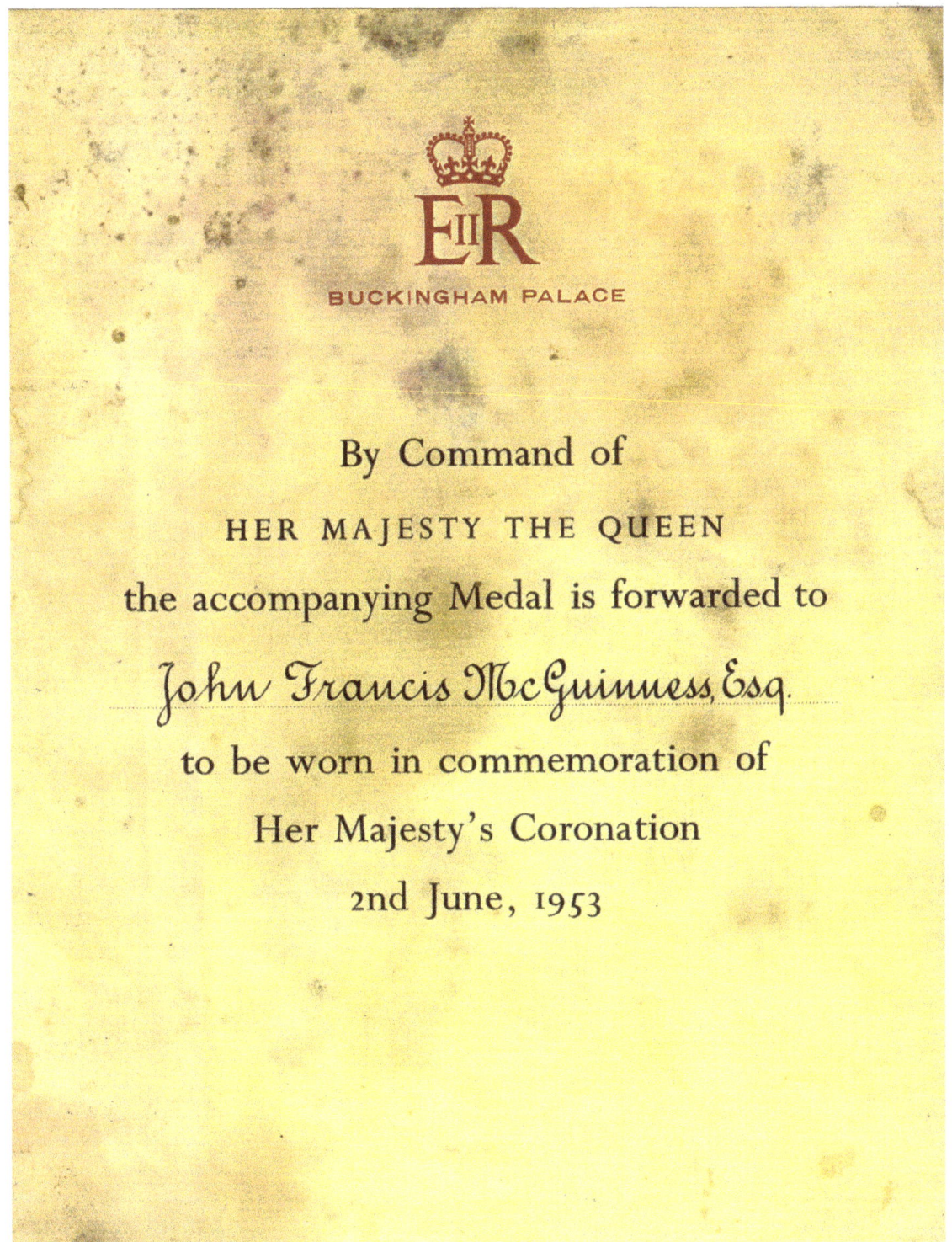

Jungung

both left and right election tickets in 1951 to ensure he gained NAWU support for is campaign for citizenship rights by 1955 his affiliations were clear. Kathy Mills recalls that 'Jack could smell a commo a mile away'.[83] A 1957 national *People* Magazine feature was headlined 'Jack McGinness Keeps The Reds Down-and out.'[84] Jack held the position of NAWU President 1955-56 to 1957-58 and 1962-63.[85]

Jack's Final Years

In the late 1950s Jack moved into an NT Administration home at 6 Stretton Street, Ludmilla. He lived with, and was primary carer for, Lucy *Ulñyunduboo* until her death in 1961.[86] His long-time work and activist colleague Babe DeMaso lived in the house opposite. It was also in walking distance to the Railway Workers Club and Railway houses in Parap where many of his former work colleagues lived. The Dowling family hotel in Parap was also nearby providing another watering hole he could catch up with mates for a drink and a chat.

Ulñyunduboo later in life while living with Jack.
(Unknown, Mills Collection).

Kathy and her husband David also shared with Jack for a time. In his retirement Jack was keen gardener, loved playing darts and enjoyed fishing trips to Buffalo

Creek where he could throw his net as he had in years gone by. Jack was also an active member of the Royal Antediluvian Order of Buffaloes(RAOB) Lodge, where he had held almost every possible position in the organisation.[87]

Jack had many lifelong friends. He was a believer that 'True friends are like diamonds: precious and rare.' One such friend was Stan Vincent who was also a member of the Royal Antediluvian Order of Buffaloes Lodge. Kathy wrote this tribute to their friendship.

> Stan came to live in Darwin after the war and became a very well respected man in the Top End communities of Katherine and Darwin. He was a very tall man, well-dressed with a strong character. That is how he stood and he was very well respected for his jolly nature and generosity that was far reaching. Jack and Stan were very good friends as they were involved in the union movement while working for the advancement of Part Aboriginal people. They drank together at the old Workers Club in Cavanaugh Street, and many good times were enjoyed in the Green Terrace Hall near the Daly Street Bridge where Jack was a Grand Member of the Antediluvian Order of Buffaloes. The McGinness family called Stan uncle because of his relationship with Aunty Ruth Williams who was related through kinship to Val's first wife Bella Humes and her brother Jim Wesley. Stan was subjected to the same regime of the Assimilation Policy of The *Native Affairs Act* and survived to also become a very good tradesman. He was a butcher by trade and he worked for Koolpinya Kool Stores in Darwin and Cowboy Collins Butcher Shop in Katherine which were the major traders with Berrimah and Rapid Creek butcher shops in the northern suburbs. His friends and customers enjoyed his bubbly nature and gentleman's approach and many recall the off-cuts as extra additions for the cat. One could not be blamed for thinking that the population was overrun by cats. Uncle Stan was a man of principle and never failed to express his sadness of the passing of his mate Jack for whom he had the greatest respect. This tribute to Uncle Stan is written with mutual love and respect. They may now together roam the pastures of the Royal Antediluvian Order of Bullaloes.

---

87 The Royal Antediluvian Order of Buffaloes is a fraternal lodge originating in the United Kingdom to provide aid to its members, their families, dependents of former members, and other charitable organisations.

Jungung

Jack McGinness at a ROAB dinner wearing his regalia, c1959. (Unknown, Mills Collection).

Jack McGinness with his ROAB darts team, c 1960. L-R: Chico Motlop, unknown, Peter Talbot, Babe Damaso, John Saxby, Jimmy Wallace, Jack McGinness. (Unknown, Mills Collection).

Jack McGinness had been a worker all his life and 'retirement' did not come easily to him. After Jack left Works and Housing in the 1960s, he returned to the railways and resumed his position as Ganger on the south gang at 22 Mile Siding, presently known as Wishart Siding. He was later recalled to assist with the laying of the rail track that was being extended on to the wharf itself.

A 2002 letter from Des Smith, a work colleague of Jack's, to Mim McGinness provides an insight to this period of time and the esteem that others felt for Jack.

> Dear Mrs McGuiness
>
> It was a pleasure to meet and talk to you and your sister Kath for a little time at Katherine a couple of weeks ago, at the railway track laying function. At the time your father's name was fresh in my mind because it had come up in a conversation I had recently had with Bob Clements, who was once a railway Ganger and later Road master on the old North Australia Railway.
>
> It was a long time ago that I knew Jack McGuiness, but across those years I remember him as a decent man who stood straight and spoke quietly, and was well respected. I met him first in 1954 when he worked as a bridge carpenter with Department of Works at the Town Yard down near the old Darwin railway station. He worked on the building of the Stokes Hill wharf, and I spent a little time as a very young engineer on that job.
>
> I still have a vividly clear memory of an occasion in 1954 when Jack was involved in an accident on the Stokes Hill wharf construction. He was on a small scaffold at the top of one of the piles when a crane hook swung and made him fall onto a barge on the water below. He was only shaken up, with a few bruises, and was lucky not to have been more badly hurt. I drove him up to the Darwin hospital to be checked for injuries.
>
> I left Darwin and the Department of Works at the end of 1955, to join Commonwealth Railways at Port Augusta. That job took me back to Darwin a few times during the 1960's, and I remember seeing Jack McGuiness again, working then in the 22-Mile gang on the North Australia Railway.
>
> My last memory of him was in January-February 1967 when I spent a few weeks on the old railway, helping out with lots of trouble on the old track, mainly between Darwin and Adelaide River.
>
> We often had all of the local gangs working together. It was a very wet period, and I remember one day down between Batchelor and Stapleton where we had a train held up with track damage to fix. It was raining heavily, and I was concerned that the men might not be able to have a hot cup of tea. Jack McGuiness went to put the billy on, and one of the engine drivers said to me "Don't worry, that man he could light a fire in the middle of a lake."[88]

---

88 McGinness, Mim, Letter written, 26 April 2002. Mills, Kathy, Personal Collection.

Jungung

Jack McGinness's interest and involvement in Aboriginal Affairs did not wane in later life. Following the 1967 Referendum and the granting of full Citizenship Rights for Aboriginal people of Australia, Jack received a Commendation Certificate and Medal from the Queen. The Medal has since been lost and the family feels it fitting that it be replaced as Jack's contribution to the Aboriginal and the wider community is something to be noted.

Jack's health deteriorated in the late 60s and early 70s due to emphysema. Jack had smoked 'rollies' throughout his life. His doctor had warned Jack that he could not help him if he did not give up. Although Jack acknowledged that he was 'proper no good' because of the 'rollies' he did not give up.[89]

Jack passed away in Darwin Hospital, Tuesday 6 March 1973. His obituary in the NT News was headlined, 'Jack McGinness: A Fighter for the Rights of Others.'[90]

Kathy felt that it was somewhat ironic that Jack's life ended in the old Darwin Hospital at Myilly Point, the very site where the Kahlin Compound previously stood. Kahlin was the birth place of Jack's political career and his life as a leader of his tribe ended. During World War 11 the site was chosen as an army hospital and after the war it remained as Darwin's hospital where life for thousands of Territorian began and ended.

Following the relocation of the hospital to the northern suburbs the site became Darwin's first University. If irony is a consequence of providence then therein lies the question, What cultural significance does this site protect for the Traditional Owners the Larrakia people? It would be of great interest to explore the creation story and in doing so it may well disclose it's true significance and revival story.

---

89 Mills, Kathy, personal communication with Matthew Stephen, 29 March 2019.
90 *NTN*, 8 March 1973.

Epilogue: Jack McGinness's Legacy

By Matthew Stephen

Ted Egan, AO, is an Australian National Living Treasure and a Territory Icon. He arrived in Darwin in 1949 and has lived in the Northern Territory ever since. Ted was a renowned sportsman in his youth and a musician throughout his life, both activities that bought him into contact with generations of the McGinness family. He has produced thirty albums and written ten books on Australian history. In 2014 he received Lifetime Achievement Award from the Tamworth Country Music Festival. He served as Administrator of the Northern Territory, 2003 to 2007. His most recent Northern Territory history is *Gilruth: A Complex Man*.[91]

Such was the relationship between Ted and the McGinness family he was bestowed the title *"Kwarak Namiook"* (Senior Man of Song). This title was bestowed on Ted in 1988 as an expression of gratitude and recognition by Valentine McGinness on behalf of his brothers and sister for the song *"Ulynindubu"* which Ted wrote as a tribute to their mother. Valentine was terminally ill at the time and knew he would not be returning home to Darwin. Before he left to join his family, who was living in Cairns North Queensland, he anxiously called for Ted to visit him in hospital so that he could name him properly (in person).

Jungung

Ted Egan, Kathy & Ali Mills, at a Friends of Kahlin event at Browns Mart, August 2013. (Koser, Di., Koser Collection).

When asked to contribute to this book with some of his experiences with Jack McGinness and his family he was happy to do so.[92]

> I became aware of the McGinness family over seventy years ago. On arrival in Darwin in 1949, I immediately became immersed in sport, mainly as a result of meeting Ron Chin – better known as Ah Hoong Ah. He was a fifth generation ABC (Australian Born Chinese) nicknamed "The Flying Chinaman". We had a common interest, Aussie Rules football. Ron played for a team called Buffaloes, as a wingman, where his pace and skill became the reason for his nickname. He quickly introduced me to various members of the team, including the captain of Buffs, the admirable Steve Abala.

---

92   Egan, Ted, email to Matthew Stephen, 22 May 2019. Note that Ted's original spelling has been retained.

Epilogue: Jack McGinness's Legacy

Steve Abala explained to me that his Mum – Bertha – had separated from his father, Barney McGinness and was now the partner of Paul Abala, so she used the name Bertha Abala. In deference to his Mum, Steve adopted the new surname. He was nonetheless a vital member of the extensive McGinness family.

At the same time I became aware of a magnificent elderly woman I saw walking, every day, from Bullocky Point into the small town of Darwin, past the Botanic Gardens. You could not miss this majestic figure. She resided in the ruins of the huge Vesteys meatworks that had been built during the years of World War One (1914-1918) – on the site nowadays occupied by the Darwin High School.

Everybody in Darwin knew the woman. Her name was Lucy McGinness. She used to stride, imperiously, into town, waving to all and sundry. She was tall, jet black, straight as a spear shaft, usually wore a big hat and often puffed contentedly on a pipe as she walked.

Portrait of Alyandabu by Robert Ingpen, 1987.
(NTL, Framed Works Collection).

I quickly established that she was Steve Abala's paternal grandmother. I began to see her quite often at social gatherings around the Police Paddock and the 118 Camp at Parap. About fifty Sidney Williams huts – erected by the defence forces during World War Two and thereafter – were used to accommodate the mixed-descent First Australian families. Steve and his wife Lorna Abala lived at No. 5 Hut at 118 and often I would camp overnight with them after a party.

It wasn't long before I was familiar with the entire McGinness family and their history. Lucy McGinness was a *Khungarakung* woman of the full descent. Her traditional name was *Alyandabu*. She was a survivor of one of the many genocidal atrocities of the era. In the late 1890s her people had been given the sinister "gift" of poisoned flour by a group of white prospectors who had ventured into the Finniss River country – south of Darwin. Many members of her tribal people died from eating the poisoned flour dampers and some of the survivors were shot by police sent to "protect" the prospectors. *Alyandabu* escaped, with a few elders.

She had good reason to hate white people, but, at age around seventeen she met and (atypically) married a young white man who had come to the Top End as an adventurer. He was an Irishman named Stephen McGinness and he had taken a job as a "snake charmer" – a fettler on the North Australian Railway that ran from Darwin to Pine Creek, later to Katherine. They were married at St Mary's Church, Darwin.

Alyandabu and Stephen McGinness lived at various railway camps and they enjoyed good relationships with all and sundry. They eventually had five children – Jack, Barney, Margaret, Valentine and Joe. In the awareness that the lives of their children would be "different", the parents raised them assiduously in two cultures. McGinness, a learned man, taught his children to speak, read and write in English. *Alyandabu* taught them the *Khungarakung* language and instructed them extensively in bushcraft and local knowledge.

On one occasion a group of men were discussing the mineral, tin, which was in high demand. *Alyandabu* told them that that was the mineral sought by the prospectors who had poisoned her people. She took McGinness to her home country, the Finniss River and showed him impressive deposits of tin. He decided to resign from the railway and they moved to the site with their children. They registered the mineral claim as The Lucy Mine: since their marriage *Alyandabu* was known in western society as Lucy McGinness.

Life progressed happily at the Lucy Mine. The family mined tin, which was in demand around World War I. The children were instructed to be proud of their dual heritage. But in 1918 there was an accident and Stephen McGinness died from gangrene. Without her white husband, at that point *Alyandabu* again was classified as a non-citizen. Her rights to the Lucy Mine were forfeited. It was the time of the White Australia Policy and Aboriginals were not counted in the census figures. It was also Government policy to remove lighter skinned children of mixed race to institutions, a sinister process – of supposed concern that "the children be given a better chance in life". It was much more sinister than that.

Jack, Margaret and Barney were old enough to stand on their own feet and get jobs, but Valentine and Joe were taken from *Alyandabu* and placed in Kahlin Home for Half-caste Children. Many tribal women never saw their children again. But *Alyandabu* was a woman of immense spirit and she went to Darwin – foreign country to her – to be near her two younger boys. Eventually she was able to regain custody of the boys and remained working in Darwin, while the boys went to school.

Jack McGinness began work on the North Australian Railway. He was an impressive man in every respect. He was tall, handsome, a fine worker, good at sport and articulate in English as well as *Khungarakung*. He was accepted as a member of the North Australian Workers Union (NAWU) in a town where unions were a formidable force. He concentrated on getting better wages and conditions for men and women like himself, First Australians of mixed descent.

Jack and his brothers were great Aussie rules footballers and they were prominent in the Vesteys team, 1918-1927, that had great success from the start of Aussie rules in Darwin in 1917, and in Buffaloes teams 1930-1942. The McGinness name is synonymous with the Darwin 'Buffaloes' football club to the present day.

Because it was officially considered that "full blooded" Aboriginals were from an inferior race, people of mixed descent were encouraged and given some incentive to align with the non-Aboriginal side of their genetic background. Most did that vehemently, often sadly severing links with the Aboriginal component of their make-up. The McGinness family was loyal to its Irish forbears, but alive and still forceful among them was their magnificent mother, *Alyandabu*, who at all times insisted that while she and her family sought good relationships with all other parties in Northern Territory society, she derived from the original owners and custodians of this land, and so did her children, and their children.

Jack McGinness and others were prominent in the establishment of a body called the AHPA – the Australian Half-caste Progressive Association, around 1950. They sought equality before the law for their members and a practice developed whereby people could apply for "exemption" from the *Aboriginals Ordinance* that had been in existence from 1911, when the Commonwealth Government took control of the Northern Territory. Jack McGinness was president of the AHPA.

The much maligned Paul (later Sir Paul) Hasluck was Minister for Territories in the early 1950s and formed a strong friendship with Jack McGinness, Babe Damaso, Tim Angeles and other leaders of AHPA. As a consequence of their discussions, Hasluck set NT Chief Clerk Jack Huthnance on the task of framing legislation to cover "assistance" to people on the basis not of their race, but of their "inability, without assistance, adequately to manage their own affairs". It was aimed absolutely at "full blood" Aboriginals nonetheless. Eventually the *Welfare Ordinance* was introduced and, at that point, around 15,000 Aboriginals of the full descent were declared to be "wards within the meaning of the *Welfare Ordinance*". So a rose was yet a rose: all "full blood" Aboriginals were still deemed – with a few exceptions, like *Alyandabu*, Albert Namatjira, Smiler Major and several others – to require "protection". Simultaneously, people of mixed Aboriginal descent were free from all the provisions of the new – still discriminatory – law.

It took only a few more years, fortunately, for all NT laws based on race to be repealed and Jack McGinness must be given due credit for his major role in the positive development of the Northern Territory, particularly in the field of race relations.

Jack, guided at all times by his parents, was undoubtedly the family's first mover and shaker. But there has been a total inheritance and the extended McGinness family is – and always will be – a force for good, particularly in the Northern Territory. They have provided wonderful initiatives in political activity, sport and music. They are determined that their unique heritage is understood among themselves and thereby they give an admirable lead for all Territorians to follow. They are determined that study and research of the *Khungarakung* language will continue. There has always been a love of crosswords and music in the family, as a consequence of Stephen McGinness's Irishness. They have always been – and will continue to be – talented and prominent, in all sports, in the most admirable manner.

In August 1918, shortly after her father's death, Margaret McGinness aged sixteen, married Harry Edwards. I suspect that *Alyandabu* would have been the matchmaker? It was a fine marriage and Margaret's children have retained a determined interest in the family's *Khungarakung* inheritance. Joe (*Pumeri*) McGinness wrote a lovely book titled *Son of Alyandabu*: Joe had an impressive Army record in World War II and, as one of the founders of FCAATSI, was instrumental in getting the 1967 Referendum passed by the biggest majority in Australia's history. Val McGinness's songs are loved by all who hear them. Val's music has been perpetuated by his brother Jack's daughter Kath, her husband David Mills and their family. They have added their own compositions: songs like Kath's "Arafura Pearl" are gems indeed.

> Yes, the McGinness Family is here to stay.
>
> I am thrilled with my own connection to the family: my song "Alyandabu" prompted the honorific "*Namiuk Kwaruk*" so I am proud to be Ted Egan AO NK. When I was Administrator of the NT (2003-2007) I implemented the Steve Abala Sporting Role Model Award: each year a Top End athlete – females and males in alternate years – is awarded the Administrator's Medal. The basis of the Award is "an illustrious sporting career and an impeccable lifestyle". The Award is retrospective to 1947.

Ted's contribution highlights that Jack McGinness's contribution to Australian and Northern Territory history should be better known and acknowledged. As a human rights activist and union leader he has few peers. Perhaps the greatest legacy of his lifetimes work is his family and the generations of social and political activists who continue the fight for human rights and social and political equality. Whether it is land rights, human rights, health, education or the environment, generations of McGinness's and the extended family have been advocates for change and reform. More often than not Kathy Mills will be front and centre advocating for the cause and supporting her family's endeavors.

Kathy is a humble and generous person. As Ted Egan points out, amongst her many achievements is that she wrote *Arafura Pearl*, which for many is the unofficial anthem and soundtrack to the history of Darwin and the Top End. In an illustration of the continuing family tradition her daughter, Ali gave a new life to her Uncle Val's Kriol version of *Waltzing Matlida* as *Waltjim Bat Matilda*. The songs exemplify how stories, history, language and culture merge seamlessly while bringing greater harmony to the community.

In working together on this book Kathy was insistent that it was a tribute to her father Jack who she always believed deserves greater acknowledgement and recognition for his role in Territory history. As has can be seen there is no denying this but nor can it be denied that Kathy is very much her father's daughter who has made her own invaluable contribution to Northern Territory Society.

While Kathy will never seek accolades for herself she cannot stop others from acknowledging her achievements. In the final stages of the preparation of this book Kathy was awarded an Order of Australia for services to the Indigenous community. The citation supporting her award lists just some of her achievements.

- Mrs Mills is a *Kungarakañ* woman and *Gurindji* Elder.
- Indigenous advocacy and welfare

Jungung

- Member, Cultural Education Team, Northern Territory General Practice Education, since 2008.
- Campaigner, 1967 Referendum.
- Activist for Indigenous rights, health and social welfare, since the 1960s.
- First woman elected to the Northern Land Council.
- Founding Member, FORWAARD Aboriginal Corporation (Foundation of Rehabilitation with Aboriginal Alcohol Related Difficulties), 1967.
- Former Delegate, Advisory Council, National Archives, 7 years.
- Member of the Stolen Generation.
- Stolen Generation, Former Board Director and Member, Elders Advisory Committee, NT Stolen Generations Aboriginal Corporation.
- Former Co-Chair for the Northern Territory Panel, Stolen Generations Inquiry.
- Involved with the production of the 'Bringing them Home' report.
- Poet, musician and singer.
- Inducted into the Northern Territory Indigenous Music Hall of Fame, 2005.
- Aboriginal of the Year, NAIDOC Awards, 1987.

Jungung is the story of Jack McGinness told through the eyes of Kathy Mills. It stands alone as a tribute to a life well lived; a life dedicated to family, community and justice. The Northern Territory has many great families whose family's contribution demands a family history. This account is just one chapter in the McGinness family history that is yet to be written.

Kathy Mills on the announcement of her receiving an Order of Australia Medal, 2019. (ABC News).

Kathy's Final Word

The door is open for change and recognition of the rights of Australia's First Nations people but it remains elusive. The door has been open before only to be closed again. All Australians have to be willing to embrace the change and work together. The fight for rights has been a long struggle but it has to continue. I'm proud that my parents instilled in me the strength to fight for our rights and persevere and that I continue my father's legacy. Although my parents were part of the Stolen Generation they were very strong in giving all our family our culture, even though they had to do it in secrecy during the years under the *Aboriginal Ordinance* and the assimilation policy.

A shared National history can be good for all of us. It's not about blame or shame, it is about truth and justice and what is the right thing to do as a nation. Once the truth is established, justice is a matter of course and other good things can happen for the people and the nation.

Jungung

Northern Lady
Pit Perrimunj (the sun going down)

Beautiful Prima Donna, reliable supreme,
The Leading lady of our Northern Screen
Her character changes are vivid and extreme
As she rules with stern reason, this Cosmic Queen.

Softly she draws back the covers from her eastern way
To introduce the world to a perfect day.
The birds are the first to stir in their nests
While the world awakens to her gentle request.

Sometimes like a fireball she crosses the sky
On hot steamy days, when the season is dry
Like a sponge that draws moisture, her demands are so high
And we may curse her harshness – for fear we may die.

Then relenting, she mellows at the end of the day
And we know it's her right – it's her mothering way.
She draws back the covers, her prelude to night
The brilliant display reveals a magnificent sight.

The vibrant colours of a northern sky
Set the stage for a final curtain and her special goodnight-
The sun setting over a crystal sea,
Is a tribute to her magnificent artistry.

So deftly she waves the silken threads
In a patchwork of colours that shows the spread
Of indigos, greys and soft pink hues
A glimpse into her palace – her most private suite.

She cast her own shadow to herald the night,
Then she lights her lantern that shines so bright.
The moon glows softly over land and sea,
Signals the end of her daily repertory.

Epilogue: Jack McGinness's Legacy

Then she pulls down the curtain when evening is nigh
Birds flutter in their nests, while others lie.
Waiting for her to call from her eastern lair
Calling to her audience her performance to share.

Sometimes she lingers before she goes to rest,
Flaunting her beauty on the ocean's crest,
She poises on the horizon as if waiting it seems,
For some sort of commitment from her ocean of dreams.

Like a mother kissing her children goodnight,
She kisses the earth before dropping out of sight.
The day concedes with the arrival of night
With her promise of safekeeping till the morning is light.

The sea responds. Its motions calms.
Soft sand glistens and waits the command
To begin its own role, its pollution plan.
As it washes the debris onto the land.

But when fires burn and scorch the earth,
It is said she's a temptress – it's for her own mirth
A scarlet lady with unquenchable thirst
Red as the devil – Death is her curse.

She burns so red as if she will burst
And the haze that surrounds her is misty with dust.
She smoulders with anger – she knows it's not right.
And she will make the difference – she will make it right.
Then she beckons the rain clouds to cover the sky.
She summons the thunderbolt to part the sky.
She peeps from behind a nimbus wall
Through a gold rimmed porthole, she'll watch over us all.

The signal of old she endorses with zest,
The colours of the rainbow is her own bequest.
She uses the colours from her special palate,
And paints the sky for the promise to be kept
Koongurrukuñ people say "She is heavy with child"

Jungung

As she labours her way across the open sky.
She is going to *Topatinj* to give life to her child.
The special place where *Wokuks* hide –

Her child the moon will be born that night
And will follow his mother on her western flight.
He will return to her womb before the morning shines bright,
To await his rebirth the following night.

The laws of *Mookanunganuk* summons her – she must obey
The survival of life she holds in her sway.
The kookaburra waits to herald the birth
Of a new day dawning – Listen for his voice.

Mooradoop Kathleen M Mills 1992.
Excerpt *Koongurrukuñ* Story *"Pitt Perramunj"* (Sun going down / Sun Setting)

Topatinj = Women's place
Wokuks = children
Mookanunganuk + the Water lily

Epilogue: Jack McGinness's Legacy

Water Lily by June Mills.

Jungung

Top a Tinj

This sacredness for land we hold
Is sacred to our very soul.
It is the source from which we came
And to that source we will return again.
The spirit of the land conducts this ancient law
As they instruct
Our future generations keep
The place where they placed their feet
And that might be a certain tree
Or a rock
Or a spring – but in reality
It is the source of life within the object holds
As our heart beats, so our life unfolds.

Top a tinj is a woman's place – and
We dare not disgrace
By pointing
Or calling out
But to keep its secrets whereabouts

We ask you – please do not stare
And to accept that place is there
Women only may speak its name
Or visit the site where our womanhood came.

This poem was written by Kathy following the Finniss River Land Claim 1981 to try and explain the sensitivity of having to give evidence and to reveal to men a sacred women's place.

Epilogue: Jack McGinness's Legacy

As we bring Jack's story to a close solace for Jack's family lies in the belief of *Koongurrukuñ* people that his spirit has returned to his tribal resting place, the Big Paperbark and his journey back through his beloved motherland to claim his status as a *Numendirk*.

Kimak

Mumuk	Farewell
Peberr-urra-ngutumu-kingoong.	We are will meet again
Wowook gini Kingulawiy	Child of Jack
Kingi neerebagini Mooradoop	Name identifying self and position

Bibliography

Archival and Library Sources

National Archives of Australia

Edwards, Gilbert Henry Langdon. Private. 'Australian Military Forces, Australian Imperial Force, Attestation Paper of Person Enlisted for Service Abroad, Canberra, 1915. Series no. B2455, barcode 1934815.

Northern Territory Archives Service (NTAS)

Oral History Interviews,

Clarke, S, Oral History Interview with Di Koser, 2000, NTRS 226 TS920.

Ludwig, Vic, Oral History Interview by Di Koser, NTRS 226 TS 950.

Mills, Kathy, Oral History Interview, by Matthew Stephen. NTRS 3163 BWF 25_S2_2.

Mills, Kathy, Oral History Interview, by Matthew Stephen. NTRS 3163 BWF_26_3_1.

State Library of the Northern Territory (NTL).

Military Units Index

http://www.ntlexhibit.nt.gov.au/items/show/1352_accessed20052019

Parliamentary and Government Sources

Commonwealth

Toohey, John. *Finniss River Land Claim*. Canberra: Australian Government Publishing Service, 1981.

Northern Territory Administrators' Reports

Spencer, Baldwin. 'Preliminary Report on the Aboriginals of the Northern Territory.' In *Northern Territory of Australia, Report of the Administrator*, CPP, 45/1913, Melbourne: Government Printer of Victoria, 1913.

Northern Territory Government

Heritage Branch. *Kahlin Compound: Background Historical Information*, November, 2009.

Personal Communications

Egan, Ted. Personal communication, email to Matthew Stephen, 22 May 2019.

Jong, Siausa. NT Births, Deaths & Marriage, Personal communication, telephone conversation, 15 May 2019.

Kathy Mills. Personal communication with Matthew Stephen, 19 January 2009.

Mills, Kathy. Personal communication with Matthew Stephen, 29 March 2019.

Mills, Kathy. Personal communication with Matthew Stephen, 24 May 2019.

Unknown. NT Births, Deaths & Marriage, Personal communication, telephone conversation, 30 April 2019.

Unpublished Papers

Brian, Bernie. 'The Northern Territory's One Big Union. The Rise and Fall of the North Australian Workers' Union 1911–1972,' PhD Thesis, Charles Darwin University, 2001.

McGinness, Mim. Letter written, 26 April 2002. Mills, Kathy, Personal Collection.

Tatz, C. 'Aboriginal Administration in the Northern Territory of Australia,' PhD Thesis, Australian National University, 1964.

Photograph Collections

Citations; Title (Creator / Institution / Collection / Reference number)

Most of the photographs in this book come from private collections. The majority belong to the Kathy Mills family collection. Thank you to Johnny Bayliss, Brenda Croft, Francine Chinn, Di Koser, the Museum and Art Gallery of the Northern Territory, David Pollock, Barbara Raymond and Ian Redpath for also lending images for use in this publication.

Photographs & images were also drawn from public collections.

NTAS	Northern Territory Archives Service
NTAS GPC	Government Photographers Collection
NTDIPL	Northern Territory Department of Infrastructure Planning and Logistics
NTL	Northern Territory Library

Published Work

Internet/Electronic Resources (www.)

Commonwealth

Australian Broadcast Corporation

Steven Schubert. *World War II attacks outside of Darwin need more recognition, historians say*

https://www.abc.net.au/news/2017-02-16/call-for-more-recognition-of-wwii-attacks-outside-of-darwin/8275498_accessed24012019

Australian National University

Indigenous Australia

http://ia.anu.edu.au/biography/mcginness-joseph-daniel-joe-17813_accessed01042019

Australian War Memorial

https://www.awm.gov.au/articles/encyclopedia/homefront/reserved_occupations_accessed14032019.

National Archives of Australia, Research Guides.

Evacuation of women and children from Darwin, 1941–42,

http://guides.naa.gov.au/records-about-northern-territory/part1/chapter4/4.2.aspx_accessed 06022019

Northern Territory Government (NTG)

Place Names Register.

Stuart Highway

https://www.ntlis.nt.gov.au/placenames/view.jsp?id = 7966_accessed21052019

Other

Soapy Vallence. http://www.blueseum.org_accessed29112018

Austin, Maisie. *A Brief History of Basketball In Darwin.* http://websites.sportstg.com/assoc_page.cgi?c = 1-166-0-0-0&sID = 329248_accessed13092018

Newspapers

Centralian Advocate (CA) 1947 – Current.

People Magazine, 1950 – Current.

The Age, 1854-1954.

The Argus 1848-1957.

The Maritime Worker, 1938-1954.

The Northern Standard, (NS) 1921–1942, 1945–1954.

Northern Territory News, (NTN) 1952- Current.

Northern Territory Times and Gazette, (NTTG) 1873–1932.

Books and Journals

Books

Austin, Maisie. *The Quality of Life: A Reflection of Life in Darwin during the Post-War Years.* Darwin: Colemans, 1992.

Austin, Tony. *I Can Picture the Old Home So Clearly: The Commonwealth and 'Half-Caste' Youth in the Northern Territory 1911–1939.* Canberra: Aboriginal Studies Press, 1993.

———. *Never Trust a Government Man: Northern Territory Aboriginal Policy 1911–1939.* Darwin: Northern Territory University Press, 1997.

Bandler, Faith. *Turning the Tide: A Personal History of the Federal Council for the Advancement of Aborigines and Torres Strait Islanders.* Canberra: Aboriginal Studies Press for the Australian Institute of Aboriginal Studies, 1989.

Bauman, Toni. *Aboriginal Darwin: A guide to Exploring Important Sites of the Past & Present.* Canberra: Aboriginal Studies Press, 2006.

Bisa, D. *Remember Me Kindly: A History of the Holtze Family in the Northern Territory.* Darwin: History Society of the Northern Territory, 2016.

Bishop, Ida Koormundum. *Nguñ Koongurrukuñ:* Speak *Koongurrukuñ.* Perth: Ida M. Bishop, 2000.

Bray, George, Laughton, Kenny & Foster, Pat. *Aboriginal Ex-Servicemen of Central Australia.* Alice Springs: Institute of Aboriginal Development, 1995.

Cramp, Norman. *Worth Fighting For: Territorian Indigenous Military Service From the Great War to Vietnam.* Darwin: Darwin Military Museum, 2018.

De La Rue, Kathy. *The Evolution of Darwin: A History of the Northern Territory's CapitalCity During the Years of South Australian Administration.* Darwin: CharlesDarwinUniversity Press, 2004.

De La Rue. *A Stubborn City: Darwin 1911-1978.* Darwin: Historical Society of the Northern Territory, 2017.

Egan, Ted. *The Role Models: Steve Abala Top End Role Models*, Darwin: Uniprint, 2006.

———. Gilruth: *A Complex Man, John Anderson Gilruth*. Alice Springs; Ted Egan Enterprises, 2017.

Farram, S. *Charles James Kirkland: The Life and Times of a Pioneer Newspaperman in the Top End of Australia*. Darwin: Uniprint, Charles Darwin University, 2017.

Gorman, S. *Legends: The AFL Indigenous Team of the Century*. Canberra: Aboriginal Studies Press, 2011.

Ogden, Pearl. *Women of Katherine*. Darwin, Pearl Ogden, 1994.

Ogden, Pearl. *Katherine's Wartime Years, 1942 to 1947*. Darwin, Pearl Ogden, 2007.

Portelli, Alessandro. *The Death of Luigi Trastulli and Other Stories: Form and Meaning in Oral History*. Albany: State University of New York Press, 1991.

Powell, Alan. *Far Country: A Short History of the Northern Territory*. Melbourne: Melbourne University Press, 2000.

———. *The Shadow's Edge: Australia's Northern War*. Revised edition. Darwin: Charles Darwin University Press, 2007.

Reed, M & Croft, S. *The Fall of the Daisy Cutters: Bombing of Katherine WWII 1939-1945*. Katherine: Katherine Historical Society, 2017.

Stephen, Matthew. *Contact Zones: Sport and Race in the Northern Territory, 1869- 1953*. Darwin: Charles Darwin University Press, 2010.

———. 'Darwin Oval, Field of Dreams, Battleground for Rights. Australian Rules Football, in Darwin, 1916–1942,' *Oral History Association of Australia Journal* 9 (2007): 1–10.

———. *Colour Bar: Remembering and Forgetting Northern Territory Football: 1916-1955*. Darwin: Uniprint, 2015.

Journals

Stanton, Sue. 'The Australian Half-Caste Progressive Association: The Fight for Freedom and Rights in the Northern Territory.' *Journal of Northern Territory History*, Historical Society of the Northern Territory, 1993, Vol 4, 37–46.

Photo Collage

Page 142 Clockwise from top left

Cecilia Muir, Joan McGinness & Irene Angeles at the Sunshine Club, c1950s. (Unknown, Mills Collection).

John McGinness (Val's son), Lloyd Anning, Val McGinness, at the Darwin Town Hall, c 1960s. (Unknown, Mills Collection).

Kathy Mills with the NT Chief Minster, Claire Martin, Australia Day, 2000. (Unknown, Koser Collection).

Kathy Mills wearing her NT and National NAIDOC medals 1986. (Koser, Di., Koser Collection).

The Mills' Sisters performing on tambourine, bush bass, T-Box, guitar. L-R: Barbara; Violet; Alison; June, c1980s. (Unknown, NTL, Northern Outlook Collection, PH0391-0004).

Back row L-R; Ali, June Mills, Tina Turner, Barbara Mills and Robyn Forscutt. Front row L-R: Nick Chandler, Robbie and Mondo Mills, c1988. (Unknown, Mills Collection.)

Mills' Sisters, Barb, Mum Kathy & sister Alison, in front of promotional material for Aboriginal Health Promotion, National Campaign Against Drug Abuse - Caring and Sharing without Grog, c 1987. (Wiedemann, B., NTL, Northern Territory Government Photographer Slide Collection, PH0730-0033).

Kathy & Ali Mills, at an NLC ceremony at Nitmuluk Park, c1989. (Unknown, Mills Collection).

Page 143 Clockwise from top left

William Mc Inness and Kathy McGinness, NT Literary Awards, 2012. (Pollock, David., Pollock Collection).

Family members at the 45th Anniversary of the Wave Hill Walk Off at Daguragu (Wattie Creek), August, 2011. (Koser, Di., Koser Collection).

Kahlin Compound centenary commemoration, 25 May 2013. L-R: Nancy Croft, Barbara Raymond & Kathy Mills. (Chinn, Francine., Chinn Collection).

Mim Mc Ginness & Kathy Mills & family members at the event marking the donation of the McGinness family heirloom, the 'Kahlin Apron', to the Museum and Art Gallery of the NT, 21 October 2014. (Archibald, Jared., MAGNT Collection).

L-R; Sadie, Mim, Kathy & Joan with Kathy's award for Appreciation of Contributions by NT Stolen Generations, November 2018. (Koser, Di., Koser Collection).

The National Apology to Australia's Indigenous peoples by Kevin Rudd, Canberra, 2008. L-R: Brenda Croft, Alec Kruger, Kathy & Robert Mills & Cynthia Sariago. (Unknown, Brenda Croft Collection).

Kathy Mills reading her poem 'Looking Back' at NT Writers Week, May 2018. (Koser, Di., Koser Collection).

Jungung